To my wife:
Thank you for walking by my side through every hill and valley.
Without your love and support this book would not be a reality, thank
you, thank you, thank you! Most people will never know the true
strength and courage you show day in and day out as my wife, and
the mother to our kids. You are more than I could have asked for in
a wife, and I am honored to be on the journey with you. Here's to
dreaming God-sized dreams together, and never staying down when
we fail. I love you and thank you for everything!

To my kids, Ty and Parker:
I love you more than you know. I hope and pray you both dream
God-sized dreams and never let failure or discouragement keep you
down in this life. God is good even when life is really hard, and when
situations don't make sense, trust Him. He is still good in hard times
as well as good times. He never changes. He has a great plan for
both of your lives!
Stay close to Him and every dream will seem possible!

TABLE OF CONTENTS

FOREWORD

As a filmmaker I don't usually jump at the chance to write the forward for a book. It's not really my thing. I make movies, but in this case, I couldn't say no because of the man I know behind the scenes' page. I'm here to endorse the character of a friend and the power of his gift with story. I've been friends with Cody since we met on the set of I CAN ONLY IMAGINE in Oklahoma. He came to speak to our crew before filming one day, and that moment made its mark on my soul, an undeniable impact of a man who has sharpened me for battle every day since. In the years that have passed, I've had an inside look at his character pursuing his God-given dreams. Cody is a passionate communicator. You'll find in the pages that follow, his skill for igniting the passion that drives him using his go-to muse from the pages of scripture, a shepherd boy named David.

When you read this book, you will experience storytelling from David's life that is commonly overlooked, and you will be challenged by a man who lives what he is teaching. Like David, Cody is a warrior fighting for his dreams while serving the same God. This book will challenge you to do the same, and as a filmmaker I encourage you to experience it like you would a movie in the theater. No distractions, fully present and fully ready to experience a moment that might just shift the course of your life.

Enjoy the journey. It's going to be special.

Andrew Erwin, Filmmaker

I CAN ONLY IMAGINE
AMERICAN UNDERDOG

ACKNOW LEDGMENTS

"Rak Chazak is a book that will both challenge AND encourage you to not only dream, but to take steps in following through with and accomplishing those dreams! With a great mix of confidence and vulnerability, Cody does a wonderful job of giving us practical action steps in 'working out our faith' and clearly showing through the scriptures (specifically the story of King David) how God has plans for each of us to accomplish more than we could ever hope or imagine."

Mac Powell,
Singer,songwriter, author

"I just finished RAK CHAZAK by Cody Bobay and was fascinated as I know you will be as well. He took on the role of storyteller, weaving things from his journey and some of the life of Biblical hero, King David, and intertwining them with the reader. There is a deep message that pulls you in, but then there are assignments that make you look at your internal world and ask some deep questions. This is a book that reminds me of the feeling I had after reading Wild at Heart by masterful writer, John Eldridge. Cody has created a work that will help you go on a deeper journey and get the courage to own the Hebrew battle cry that the book is named after. Whether you read it by yourself, with your sons or father, or as a men's group or church this is a powerful tool that is going to take you on a deeper identity journey."

Shawn Bolz
Author, Social Commentator & TV Host, Minister
www.bolzministries.com

"I've never read a book like this. Cody Bobay brings to life the youthful days of King David in a masterfully relatable, deeply profound way. David is the metaphor for each one of us through which we experience a God who is keenly aware of who we are and is working on us to reach our own kingly potential. Like all inspired books I've read, Rak Chazak has a divine timeliness to it. I am a changed man for having read it."

Adam Allred
Founder of Ninefold Marketing

"In the pages of this book RAK CHAZAK you will be challenged, encouraged, and convicted to dream, prepare, and live out a lifestyle with courage for King Jesus. You will be reminded that with the strength, courage, and victory that comes from YAHWEH, you can have the mindset of the war cry RAK CHAZAK so that you can keep fighting, win today, and go light it up for the King!"

Eric Stewart
Lead Pastor Liberty Church Lula
Men of Valor Ministries Executive

"A must-read for dreamers and goal-seekers alike. Bobay brilliantly arranges a fictionalized journey of David with his personal experiences to empathize with the reader. The Rak Chazak Lifestyle is truly a model for individual growth and development."

Hector Knudsen
Entrepreneur

"I just finished reading Rak Chazak! Cody Bobay, as a behind the scenes storyteller, masterfully communicates the early life of David.

There are so many things I could say about this book.

But, when you read a book you are reading the author. This is a must read because you as the reader get to sense the heart of the author, Cody Bobay.

Cody launched himself in the face of weak, apathetic, woke Christianity. In a day and time when words like; Warrior, Kingdom, and standard are thrown around by men who haven't the slightest idea what they mean, Cody has the courage to take us on a journey of what it actually means to be a warrior for Christ furthering His Kingdom and upholding a standard.

Read this book and follow this author if you truly want to be inspired."

IV Marsh
Author and Lead Pastor, Founder Becoming Man

"What a powerful and interactive journey Cody created here with RAK CHAZAK. Not only does this book delve into the author's personal life and battles, but we can see the themes exemplified through the lenses of one of my favorite characters from the Bible, David. This book will challenge your perspective and show you how to take up this battle call on a daily basis. To walk in courage and faith, boldly. Leaning on trust in God and not having to figure out everything on your own. As a filmmaker, I like to approach creating a story in a parable-like format. This book contains great, new parables about a time in David's life that is often overlooked. Buckle up for this read and get ready to start walking in the RAK CHAZAK lifestyle."

Chase Kuker
Filmmaker II Composer
www.lunardoor.com II www.chromosomesmusic.com

"Any man with a faith in God I would implore you to read Cody Bobay's book, RAK CHAZAK.

I love the lessons Cody shares in this book, every chapter is filled with valuable teachings that all modern men need to hear and live by.

We live in a time of true uncertainty and Cody has given men a guide for how to be honorable, honest, God fearing men who love the Lord, and in his words to 'Lean into Gods chisel and trust his process'. There are many passages in this book designed to help you overcome deep wounds of the past, Cody does an amazing job showing you how you can utilize Gods love to help you heal through prayer and forgiveness.

I will be recommending this book to everyone I know. I feel the Holy Spirt when I read the passages Cody has written, and it would be irresponsible of me as a follower of Christ to not recommend this incredible work to everyone I know.

Thank you Cody for giving the world this gift."

Tyce Nielsen
Duo Transcend

"RAK CHAZAK is encouraging to me and my faith through the tough times, and this crazy world we live in. It reminded me that God is training me. These tough trials that seem like there is no way out. With a strong enough faith, the Lord will make a way. This book reminds me of my hope."

Sidney Outlaw
Bellator Fighter

NOTE TO READER

Before we kick things off, I need to honor you and set proper expectations for the journey we're about to embark upon together. I am an actor and author, but not a theologian. I love Jesus, I read His word daily, and I have followed Him whole-heartedly for over two decades. As you read this book you'll be reading the story of David in a way you probably never have before, and I want you to fully experience this narrative. Like Andy said in the foreword, experience it just like you would a movie when you go to the theater: no distractions, fully present. My goal is to draw our hearts into moments of David's humanity that we might not have thought of before, with the hope that those moments increase our passion and zeal for living out the dreams and passions God has placed in our hearts today. There will be moments in this story where David stops to worship; allow your heart to worship with him. Don't get caught up in the exact timeline of that Psalm; that's not my goal with this. My goal is to have those moments open your heart to have an experience of praise as you read through this. Read it that way and prepare your heart to experience the presence of the Lord. I truly believe you will. I worked to make sure everything is as Biblically accurate as possible, but if you're an artist of any kind, you know you must make creative choices that you hope only add to the experience and not distract from it. For example, the giants I will discuss: some people have very strong stances on if they were descendants of the Nephilim, and I respect those stances completely. For this book I made the creative choice to have Goliath a part of the Nephilim race. Again, the accuracy of his bloodline is not the main point. The point is the experience and the take-aways we will have. So allow your mind to be fully immersed in this journey, because I believe if you do, the Lord is going to use this book to do something special in your life. I love you guys, and I'm excited for the adventure you're about to take!

RAK CHAZAK

"'Be strong and courageous (chazak v'ematz). Do not be afraid or terrified because of them, for the Lord your God goes with you; he will never leave you nor forsake you.'

Then Moses summoned Joshua and said to him in the presence of all Israel, 'Be strong and courageous, for you must go with this people into the land that the Lord swore to their ancestors to give them, and you must divide it among them as their inheritance.

The Lord himself goes before you and will be with you; he will never leave you nor forsake you. Do not be afraid; do not be discouraged.'"
Deuteronomy 31:6-8 NIV

The combination of these two Hebrew words, Chazak and Amats (chazak v'ematz) were repeated amongst the Israelites simply through the war cry of "RAK CHAZAK!" Those two words spoken together were enough to cause an Israelite soldier's heart to be filled with courage and prepare for any challenge ahead of him. RAK CHAZAK roughly translates to the rock-like "oomph" of the spiritually zealous heart, the game face of a mighty warrior, tenacity of soul, the gritting of the teeth of the spirit-inspired warrior, and the baring of those teeth to the enemy. It is possessing a resolute and confident resolve for the glory of God, a rush of spiritual fervor, a tensing of every muscle.

My goal with this book is to show that each of us can have the same response to this war cry in our everyday lives. Some call things like this a mantra, and I'm a fan of some of them, but there is a big difference between a mantra and a war cry. It's time for all of us to learn the power of a war cry in our modern-day culture. It's time for us to experience a new level of courage, in our everyday lives.

INTRO DUCTION

"For I know the plans I have for you," declares the Lord, "plans to prosper you and not to harm you, plans to give you hope and a future."
Jeremiah 29:11 NIV

Before we begin, I want to tell you a few things that I believe we all need to hear from time to time. First, I am proud of you. I'm proud of you for buying a book to learn to become a more courageous person with your dreams and passions. If I would have known how difficult life was as a kid, I never would have wanted to grow up so badly. I thought life as an adult would be simple and just about having fun... Boy was I wrong. But there's a saying I love that challenges me to maximize every day: If you have breath in your lungs today, you made God's wake-up list, and every name on that list has purpose, potential, and hope for a brighter future. I am honored to be on that list with you. I hope and pray we make the most of every day we have moving forward, knowing that God loves us, He has a great plan for our lives, and that He will make all things work together for good.

"And we know [with great confidence] that God [who is deeply concerned about us] causes all things to work together [as a plan] for good for those who love God, to those who are called according to His plan and purpose."
Romans 8:28 AMP

I want you to know I wrote this book with you in mind. This book is not about David, even though we will follow a part of his life; this book is not about me, even though I will share some stories from my journey. Every word on every page is soaked in prayer and in hope that you will be impacted. That you will begin to see yourself the way God sees you and not through the lens of your past mistakes. I believe with my whole heart that, if we can catch a glimpse of how God sees us, insecurities, doubts, and fears would have to leave our hearts. If we can truly see how magnificently we were created, and how deeply we are loved, our everyday lives will be impacted from this point forward. We will truly have extraordinary courage because we will know who believes in us.

I pray RAK CHAZAK is that catalyst for you. No matter if you're old or young, I believe this book will have a special impact on your soul and thought life moving forward.

I love you. I'm proud of you. I'm excited to take this journey with you. Buckle up. It's going to be a magnificent ride.

"You're off to great places! Today is your day! Your mountain is waiting, Go, get on your way!"
Dr. Seuss

CHAPTER ONE

Big Dreams and
Humble Beginnings

"Blessed is the man who walks not in the counsel of the wicked, nor stands in the way of sinners, nor sits in the seat of scoffers; but his delight is in the law of the Lord, and on his law he meditates day and night. He is like a tree planted by streams of water that yields its fruit in its season, and its leaf does not wither. In all that he does, he prospers."
Psalm 1:1-3 ESV

As the sun crests over the horizon, a gust of wind kicks up, pushing the breeze of a new day across the terrain of Israel. Each new day brings opportunities, challenges, and, if you're not careful, moments of deep loneliness. These lands have no mercy on the unprepared, and some days, no mercy on the most prepared. As the gust of wind reaches the outcrop of trees it aggressively shakes each leaf, sending the dew plummeting to the ground.

Below one of the trees is a shepherd getting some rest after a night of watching his herd. The trees have always given him cover and protection from the threats of the land. Lying there, the dew crashes onto his forehead. The shepherd suddenly snaps to his feet and drops a stone into his sling without looking down, heart pounding and eyes scanning the area for any threats...

As he slows his breathing, he focuses on preparing for whatever threat could be out there. Standing there, he meditates on what he's learned from reading the lives of the great heroes of Israel. He pictures himself standing next to the great warlords, Joshua and Caleb, before the attack of the royal armies at the waters of Mermom. Armies that had united against Israel, that had more men than sand on the seashore. But Joshua and Caleb were men who would stand against enemies of any number and any stature because they knew Yahweh was with them. These men feared no other man, including the half-man, half-demon creatures called Nephilim.

Even the thought of the Nephilim, and how offensive they were to Yahweh, causes the shepherd to spit on the ground in disgust. The hatred for this race of people makes his blood boil…

Then it happened… The greatest moment any warrior could ask for. The calm before the storm… The feeling that battle is imminent. It's finally time. Joshua turns to the army, full of the Lord's people, and shouts with the ferocity of a lion the war cry passed down from Moses:

"RAK CHAZAK!"

The army holds up their Khopesh blades and shields in unison, shouting their war cry back to Joshua, shaking the defensive walls of the city and bringing terror to every enemy because they know what follows this war cry:

"RAK CHAZAK!"

They sprint into battle with wings of eagles, faces of lions, and hearts confident of the victory Yahweh would deliver in the face of impossible odds…

The shepherd suddenly hears a branch break in the distance; his senses heighten as he is pulled back into the reality of the moment abruptly. Something is approaching… The shepherd crouches, stone in sling, ready to sprint and destroy any threat in his path.

His muscles relax and he stands up as he realizes it's his oldest brother Eliab.

"Stop acting like a warrior, and put that stupid sling down. Our whole family knows you don't have what it takes. Just give it up. Write your songs, watch the sheep, and accept the destiny of the redheaded shepherd baby. Oh, and father wants to see you; he needs your help making some food. Some of my friends are coming over tonight and we are going to talk about serving under the greatest warrior-king these lands will ever know. We might even let you listen in, as long as you don't screw up our meal again."

The shepherd considers responding, but he's learned it only leads to a fight he cannot win. Eliab has always been bigger and stronger than any of his brothers, and he knows it. When they fight, he doesn't stop. He brings painful lessons every time. Having the heart of a warrior doesn't always translate to having the fighting skills, so he grabs his things, rouses the sheep, and begins the journey home.

Walking home the shepherd begins to weep, his feelings completely hurt by the words and actions of his brother, just now and throughout his lifetime. His family's lack of faith begins to siphon the courage out of his soul. Tears continue falling as his heart longs for genuine love and acceptance from a brother, a true friend that would love him and truly understand him. Maybe Yahweh would provide that someday…

Chapter One (b): Big Dreams and Humble Beginnings

"What lies behind you and what lies in front of you, pales
in comparison to what lies inside of you."
Ralph Waldo Emerson

As we read through this book, we will go through the fictionalized journey of David at the start of each chapter and discuss some key takeaways that I hope and pray impact your life to live every single day with extraordinary courage. My goal is that RAK CHAZAK becomes a war cry for each of us, a shout of victory before every day and challenge starts. As David remembers the stories of Joshua and Caleb, I believe we must fill our minds with the same inspiration from God's word. We live in a completely different world, but our need for a war cry to advance the Kingdom of God is just as high.

One of the greatest battlefields on which our war cry is needed is that of our minds. There is a war to truly believe that God has placed greatness inside each of us; dreams and passions to impact this world in a special and unique way based on our specific lives, giftings, and talents. If you don't believe it, let me tell you, He has! You have greatness in you given from the Lord, and there is a war for you to live that out in your life. A war full of doubts, insecurities, fears, and whispers from the Enemy that you are not enough. But hear me, this is a fight we must engage in and win in the strength and power of God! We have dreams given to us that are beyond our current skill sets and résumés. Dreams that will impact the world around us to help advance God's Kingdom. I pray as you're reading this the Lord begins to awaken those dreams and passions in a way that radically transforms your everyday life. A transformation of your heart that becomes uncontainable. We only get one chance to fully pour out our dreams and passions into this world; let's make it count. Let's dare greatly, take risks, and make sure when it's time to be with the Lord, we finish our race with a heart full of honor by knowing we gave everything we had...

"It is not the critic who counts; not the man who points out how
the strong man stumbles, or where the doer of deeds could have

done them better. The credit belongs to the man who is actually in the arena, whose face is marred by dust and sweat and blood; who strives valiantly; who errs, who comes short again and again, because there is no effort without error and shortcoming; but who does actually strive to do the deeds; who knows great enthusiasms, the great devotions; who spends himself in a worthy cause; who at the best knows in the end the triumph of high achievement, and who at the worst, if he fails, at least fails while daring greatly, so that his place shall never be with those cold and timid souls who neither know victory nor defeat."
Theodore Roosevelt

At the end of this chapter I invite you to grab a pen and paper and put today's date at the top of the journal page, then write down the dreams you believe the Lord has placed on your heart. Make sure your dreams are not limited based on your current skills, résumé, or your bank account. Personally, I love the "shot-clock timer" mentality with decisions like this. Set a "shot-clock" of 60 seconds write your dreams down, and then continue reading...

"It is God's privilege to conceal things and the king's privilege to discover them."
Proverbs 25:2 NLT

Now that you're done, take a picture of that journal page with your phone. Look at it every day until you finish this journey. You might feel embarrassed by what you wrote down, or intimidated, or it might feel completely impossible, and that's great! That's exactly why I believe the Lord has you reading this book. God's timing is perfect, and He passionately loves the details. I believe God is kinder than we all think, more precise with timing, and I also believe that He is cheering us on more than we will ever know. So, hang on to that paper, look at it, pray over it, and let me share a story of how I did the same thing almost two decades ago...

"It always seems impossible until it's done."
Nelson Mandela

I'll never forget it: I was on a deployment with the United States Navy, where I served six years as a Naval Aircrewman. We had just finished a mission and were flying back to our base with some downtime on the plane. I pulled out a pen and paper and wrote down a dream that I felt bubbling out of my heart. I wrote that I wanted to write books and speak to Christians around the world about living out their full potential. As I was writing, I began to draw a globe to help me visualize what I wrote down. I've always loved globes. Then, I made a mistake. One of the guys on the plane with me came by and asked me what I was writing and drawing, and I told him everything, thinking he would see it too and cheer me on. He didn't. It was a brutal stretch of 15-30 minutes. This wasn't a mean person, but a friend trying to talk sense into me. He wanted to talk about my dream based on the practicality of my achieving it He asked me questions like, "Do you have a degree? Have you ever written a book? Have you spoken at a church before? Have you ever done any public speaking?" I was honest with him and felt completely deflated when my answer to all of those questions was no. He felt like he did me a service, as a friend, and I felt humiliated, as if all of my courage left my soul.

I encourage you to be very careful with whom you share your dreams. I've learned the people that care the most about us will try to talk sense into us because they don't want us to get hurt and fail. The key to unlocking your dreams is not based on your current skill set, job or résumé. The key is faith.

After that flight, I had a choice to make. The words from that friend could affect my faith in my future potential. I chose what I believed God had placed on my heart. I share with you today and boast in the strength of the Lord working through me: by the time my first book released, I had finished my time in the military, completed my graduate degree, and started my full-time career of speaking at conferences, churches and events! God is so good! Impossible is truly nothing to God! And as my wife can testify, not one step was easy, but God was with me and my family, and I promise if He can do it through someone like me, He can do it through you!

"For truly, I say to you, if you have faith like a grain of mustard seed, you will say to this mountain, 'Move from here to there,' and it will move, and nothing will be impossible for you.'"
Jesus, Matthew 17:20b ESV

Date

_____

Reflections

_____

_____

_____

_____

_____

_____

_____

_____

_____

_____

_____

_____

_____

_____

_____

_____

_____

CHAPTER TWO

Facing the wounds
from our past

"He heals the brokenhearted and bandages their wounds."
Psalms 147:3 NLT

After a long trip home, still feeling the emotional fatigue of his brother's words, the shepherd is excited to see his father. It's been over a week since he left to watch the flock.

"Maybe this time will be different," the shepherd says under his breath, hopeful to have his father show him some affection and love.

Walking up to the house, Jesse rushes out with excitement.

"Son! Hurry up! It's a great day! Eliab, Abinadab, and Shammah's battle buddies are coming over and I want to prepare the best meal possible. Go out to the flock, grab a lamb, and prepare it for dinner. I am so proud of your brothers! They have become strong warriors under the great King Saul!"

Tears fill the shepherd's eyes, the reality setting in that his father has overlooked him yet again.

"Just a hug. That's all." The shepherd mumbles to himself as he walks out to do his least favorite thing: take the life of one of the sheep he protects.

Walking out to his flock, he begins to meditate again on the great warlord Joshua, thinking about how Joshua, his hero from the stories of old, began his life as a slave in Egypt. People have said Joshua was a dreamer as well; they said Joshua dreamed of leading his people to victory someday, but was ridiculed because they were enslaved under the most terrifying ruler throughout history. People told Joshua to focus on being a slave because it was his destiny, but Joshua continued to pray to Yahweh, asking Yahweh for the strength to be a faithful and strong slave until the time came for him to be a warrior.

This thought inspires the shepherd to continue to fully follow Yahweh in his heart, knowing Yahweh can do the same in him as he did for the Israelites in Egypt.

The shepherd walks over to a young lamb. He embraces him and begins to think about his presence and protection since the lamb's birth. Whether a sacrifice to Yahweh or to feed his family, he knows the purpose of killing the lamb but wants to bring comfort before death, so he gently sings to each one before they are killed. The shepherd begins to sing a song he wrote as a child when he was watching his flock in the wilderness. It comforts him in the darkest moments, and he always dreams of this song bringing comfort and hope to the Israelite people, but for now, he hopes it brings comfort to this lamb before his death:

"The Lord is my shepherd, I lack nothing. He makes me lie down in green pastures, he leads me beside quiet waters, he refreshes my soul. He guides me along the right paths for his name's sake. Even though I walk through the darkest valley, I will fear no evil, for you are with me; your rod and your staff, they comfort me. You prepare a table before me in the presence of my enemies. You anoint my head with oil; my cup overflows. Surely your goodness and love will follow me all the days of my life, and I will dwell in the house of the Lord forever."
Psalms 23:1-6 NIV

Chapter Two(b): Facing the wounds from our past

"Heal the boy and the man will appear."
Tony Robbins

This chapter is one of the most difficult to write. I know the consequences of breezing through this chapter; I've seen it first-hand and I want to encourage you not to rush this book or this chapter. I believe the Lord is going to do a work in all of us if we don't pretend like everything is okay. For the outcome of this book, my hope and prayer is that each of us learns to live the RAK CHAZAK mentality and lifestyle. A lifestyle of extraordinary courage knowing the Lord is with us and no challenge we face can overtake us. But to get there, we must allow the Spirit to do healing in our hearts.

Here's what I want you to do. We are going to do the "shot-clock" with three areas, starting with the wounds from your parents or siblings. Use the journal page at the end of this chapter, set the timer for 60 seconds, and write down an area in which you know you need healing from the Lord. Maybe your story is similar to David's and you have been neglected, overlooked, and you feel forgotten by your family. Maybe you had a great upbringing and feel embarrassed talking about the wounds because they don't seem as extraordinary as those of other people. Maybe they resemble those of the people to whom I have ministered after my book Soulcon Challenge released, with hundreds of men confessing wounds they had never shared with anyone. Wounds that were eating away at their soul. Please hear me, we all need healing. None of us were created to walk with hurt hidden in the closet of our souls. Jesus wants to help us with every single hurt. I believe extraordinary courage is only possible with genuine vulnerability before the Lord and the people we love in our lives. Start the "shot-clock" and write down the area or areas in which you need healing.

"So do not fear, for I am with you; do not be dismayed, for I am your God. I will strengthen you and help you; I will uphold you with my righteous right hand."
Isaiah 41:10 NIV

I'm proud of you. I know that is not easy. It is shocking to me how wounds from our childhood constantly impact our lives as adults. If you need to pause, reflect, or cry, please do it. I have been a Christian for over 20 years and it blows my mind that I continue to discover wounds from my childhood that need healing. I think it's one of the most courageous things we can do to write those wounds down, bring them before the Lord, and then work through them. This is a battlefield on which we need our war cry, a battlefield on which we cannot pretend ignorance will lead to victory or bliss; it never does.

Let me share a little about my journey with you in this area. I was raised by my father and saw my mother every other weekend for visitation most of my childhood. My parents never got along and fought constantly, and as a kid you deal with some difficult emotions during situations like this that you are not prepared to handle, often leaving the kid confused, hurt and feeling a weight of responsibility that is crushing to the soul. It wasn't until I was 18 that I met Jesus and started following Him. Until then, I tried to heal those wounds with the party lifestyle. Some of us have been tricked into believing this works, but it inevitably makes new wounds without healing old ones. When I was 21, I married my incredible wife, thinking I was healed from every wound and mature enough to be a healthy, whole husband to my bride. Wow, I was in for a rude awakening... I learned very quickly that the Lord works in our lives through the process of sanctification, the process that takes place throughout our entire lives to look more like Jesus and less like who we were. It's a beautiful process, but at times it is very painful, and we need the help of others to find victory in that journey. This is one of the main reasons I have the statue of David on the cover of this book.

Some say that when Michelangelo was finished creating the Statue of David he was frequently asked how he did it. His response was that it was simple: he just chipped away everything that didn't look like David. I believe the Lord is doing that in each of our lives, and that process is like art. It is detailed and not rushed, because the artist is also our creator. He knows how truly magnificent He created us to be. So let the cover of this book be a reminder to you as we continue this journey that every time you see the Statue of David moving forward;

the remembrance that God is slowly and methodically making each of us into a masterpiece. That process takes our entire lives, and it's magnificent.

Allow the Lord to do this work in your heart, no matter how painful it is. Lean into His "chisel," and trust His process. I believe on the other side is a new level of healing and victory in the Lord.

"For we are God's masterpiece. He has created us anew in Christ Jesus, so we can do the good things he planned for us long ago."
Ephesians 2:10 NLT

Before we move on to the next area, here are a few prayers I would love for you to make:

- "Lord, do I need to seek professional counseling for these wounds?" I am a massive fan of counseling. Marriage counseling at year seven saved my marriage, and I cannot recommend counseling enough. If you feel like this is your next step, don't hesitate.
- "Lord, please put on my heart a trusted friend to share this (or these) wounds with." There is healing when we sit with people we love and trust and share with them, but I think it's important to pray about the right person to share this with. This is a vulnerable thing to share and you want to make sure it's shared with the right person or people. This is such a courageous step that will bring healing and victory from these wounds having power over you. I am confident because I've seen it so many times in my life.
- "Lord, I forgive my parents or siblings (or both). Fully." Forgiveness is crucial to the healing process. Take that step of courage and forgive them, you won't regret it.

"Our Father in heaven, may your name be kept holy. May your Kingdom come soon. May your will be done on earth, as it is in heaven. Give us today the food we need, and forgive us our sins, as we have forgiven those who sin against us. And don't let us yield to temptation, but rescue us from the evil one."
Matthew 6:9-13 NLT

The second area is with the wounds from our friends. And I have to be honest, I never thought I would write part of a book about wounds from friends. I'm speaking specifically about the scars we have on our backs from the "friends" we thought would ride or die with us. Those friends that we trusted like Jesus did with Judas (the disciple that betrayed Jesus). Those wounds hurt badly and they seem to continually be ripped open in our lives when we are reminded of them.

I realized the reason I don't have many friends in my life is because I try to protect myself from new wounds happening, because those "friend" wounds hurt so badly. As I write this, I am wrestling with the thought of "who are you to write this chapter?" But I know who I am in Christ, and I spent time by my fire this morning praying and reminding myself that this book isn't about me anyway, it's about you. I am called to share and pray the Lord works in your heart like He is working in mine. My goal is for you to learn from my life, my failures, successes, and anything in between as you allow the Lord to do a work in your heart during the journey of this book. Again, start the "shot-clock" and write down the area or areas in which you need healing.

Before we move on to the next area, here are those same prayers; make them again:

- "Lord, do I need to seek professional counseling for these wounds?"
- "Lord, please put on my heart a trusted friend to share this (or these) wounds with."
- "Lord, I forgive these people (or person) for hurting me. Fully" Reminder: Forgiveness is crucial to the healing process. Take that step of courage and forgive them, you won't regret it.

"If you love deeply, you're going to get hurt badly. But it's still worth it."
C.S. Lewis

Now, for the final area: the self-inflicted wounds. These are some of the most embarrassing, painful and humiliating ones, but let me share this and I pray it sets you free: there is no shame in Christ. None. No matter what wounds you've caused, or are causing, healing is waiting and His name is Jesus. There is no sin too dark, or no sin tolerated too long, that He cannot free you from. With Soulcon Challenge I've seen men across the world freed from the painful prison of self-inflicted wounds. I want that same thing for you.

It's time; set the "shot-clock" and write down the self-inflicted wounds you have caused or maybe are still causing.

You did it. I'm proud of you. Just like before, let's pray over this and be willing to take action. Again, here are a few prayers I would love for you to make:

- "Lord, do I need to seek professional counseling for these self-inflicted wounds?"
- "Lord, please put on my heart a trusted friend to share this (or these) wounds with."
- "Lord, I know you love me and forgive me, fully. Thank you. I also choose to forgive myself, and I ask for your healing. I love you. Fully."

"For as high as the heavens are above the earth, so great is his love for those who fear him; as far as the east is from the west, so far has he removed our transgressions from us. As a father has compassion on his children, so the Lord has compassion on those who fear him; for he knows how we are formed, he remembers that we are dust. The life of mortals is like grass, they flourish like a flower of the field; the wind blows over it and it is gone, and its place remembers it no more. But from everlasting to everlasting the Lord's love is with those who fear him, and his righteousness with their children's children— with those who keep his covenant and remember to obey his precepts."
Psalms 103:11-18 NIV

"Therefore confess your sins to each other and pray for each other so that you may be healed. The prayer of a righteous person is powerful and effective."
James 5:16 NIV

Date

Reflections

CHAPTER THREE

Dealing with doubt and failure

"I am losing all hope; I am paralyzed with fear. I remember the days of old. I ponder all your great works and think about what you have done. I lift my hands to you in prayer. I thirst for you as parched land thirsts for rain. Come quickly, Lord, and answer me, for my depression deepens. Don't turn away from me, or I will die. Let me hear of your unfailing love each morning, for I am trusting you. Show me where to walk, for I give myself to you."
Psalms 143:4-8 NLT

A few weeks after the dinner, the shepherd is back in the wilderness with the sheep. The majority of his life is lived alone, and that doesn't bother him most of the time, but it can get lonely, and occasionally terrifying.

It's the middle of the day; the sheep are resting in the shade, so he pulls out his harp. He loves pouring his heart out to Yahweh in song, and he has always enjoyed writing new music, and thinks of singing these songs to encourage people to be strong and courageous for Yahweh like he hopes to be.

For his entire life, the shepherd has always had an underlying fear of certain threats, knowing without Yahweh showing up in power some of the threats could overtake him. A few weeks ago, while preparing the meal for his brothers and their battle buddies, his father told him about a lion that had devoured a few shepherds in the area.

His father said to him, "Son, you are not as strong as most young men. If you see this lion, run and hide. They have said it's the biggest lion they have ever seen and it has a taste for human blood. I know you think you're a warrior, but you are not and will never be. I want you to run if you see this lion. Do you understand?"

"Dad, if I see it I will do what Samson did! I will grab it by the mane and strike it in the face and rip it in half. I have what it takes!"

"Son, no you don't! You don't have what it takes! Will you please get that through your thick head!?! You are a musician, and built more like a woman than a man!"

Heartbroken, the shepherd wanted to honor Yahweh by honoring his father, so he just said, "yes sir."

Remembering this conversation hurt the shepherd's heart all over again. The shepherd leans back on the tree next to him and grabs his harp and begins to sing a song that really helps him in moments like this:

"The Lord is my light and my salvation— whom shall I fear? The Lord is the stronghold of my life— of whom shall I be afraid? When the wicked advance against me to devour me, it is my enemies and my foes who will stumble and fall. Though an army besiege me, my heart will not fear; though war break out against me, even then I will be confident. One thing I ask from the Lord, this only do I seek: that I may dwell in the house of the Lord all the days of my life, to gaze on the beauty of the Lord and to seek him in his temple. For in the day of trouble he will keep me safe in his dwelling; he will hide me in the shelter of his sacred tent and set me high upon a rock. Then my head will be exalted above the enemies who surround me; at his sacred tent I will sacrifice with shouts of joy; I will sing and make music to the Lord. Hear my voice when I call, Lord; be merciful to me and answer me. My heart says of you, 'Seek his face!' Your face, Lord, I will seek. Do not hide your face from me, do not turn your servant away in anger; you have been my helper. Do not reject me or forsake me, God my Savior. Though my father and mother forsake me, the Lord will receive me. Teach me your way, Lord; lead me in a straight path because of my oppressors. Do not turn me over to the desire of my foes, for false witnesses rise up against me, spouting malicious accusations. I remain confident of this: I will see the

goodness of the Lord in the land of the living. Wait for the Lord; be strong and take heart and wait for the Lord."
Psalms 27:1-14 NIV

As he finishes singing he smiles, grateful for the opportunity to sing to the Lord of Hosts, knowing He is always listening.

"RAK CHAZAK!"

The shepherd shouts!

"RAK CHAZAK!"

He shouts again, feeling like one of the warlords of old, the war cry from the Hebrew warriors that would inspire them to fight with strength and courage without even thinking of failure. His strength is coming back, and he goes to shout once more-

He hears something. Probably just his brother again, but he can't risk it, the lives of these sheep depend on it. He jumps to his feet, drops a stone in his sling, and crouches, using every sense in his body, scanning every inch in sight, trying to slow his breathing to remain as quiet as possible.

As he scans the horizon, he sees nothing. Maybe it was a gust of wind. He holds fast, breathing slowly. Nothing.

He heaves a big sigh, grabs the rock out of his sling, and turns to sit back down... In that moment, he hears it again, knowing it's not a gust of wind. He is being hunted. Terror grips his body. The words of his father race back through his head, and panic takes over. He goes to drop the rock back in his sling, but misses it because he is shaking so badly. The rock falls to the ground with a crash into the twigs below him. As if the falling rock was a signal to attack, the most terrifying thing the shepherd has ever seen leaps out of the brush across from him. This wasn't just a lion, this looks like a half-demon, half-lion, and it stands there making eye contact with the shepherd. Every audible breath of the lion sounds like a roar from the pit of hades.

Between the shepherd and the lion were the sheep. Every ounce of courage is gone, and the shepherd knows the lion can sense it. Every story of the heroes of old, every song he has sung, nothing is working in his heart.

"Yahweh, save me," he whispered with the fear and trembling of a frightened child.

Still making eye contact with the lion, fear overtakes the shepherd and he turns to run. He sprints as fast as he can to a tree he can climb and rushes up the branches, terrified.

As he reaches a height that he feels is safe, he turns back to look. Still standing in the same spot, the lion is watching him, breathing heavily and not breaking eye contact. The lion steps forward toward the sheep, but keeps his eyes locked on the shepherd.

"No!!!" the shepherd yells, but it does nothing.

The lion grabs a sheep by the neck, crunching every bone with one bite, and never losing eye contact with the shepherd as if possessed by a demon.

Completely helpless and terrified, the shepherd begins to weep for the sheep he lost and for the cowardice in his heart.

The lion walks over to the tree, the sheep dangling in the grip of his jaws. He drops the bleeding, limp sheep at the base of the tree as if to serve as a warning. The lion looks straight up and fear consumes the shepherd, who knows if the lion comes after him, he is dead. Then, surprisingly, the lion turns and walks right past the other sheep back into the brush he came from.

The reality sinks into the shepherd's heart. He failed. Miserably. He let fear control him. And now he is starting to believe he doesn't truly have what it takes...

Chapter Three (b): Dealing with doubt and failure

"Success is not final; failure is not fatal: it is the courage to continue that counts."
Winston Churchill

The reality sinks into the shepherd's heart. He failed. Miserably. He let fear control him. And now he is starting to believe he doesn't truly have what it takes…

I put this here again to make sure we didn't skip over it. I am using the life of David in this fictionalized story (though striving for biblical accuracy) and stories from my life with the goal of impact. This entire book is about impacting your everyday life. I hope it teaches you how to live with extraordinary courage; I believe to do that we need to be able to face hard things to allow the Lord to do surgery in our hearts. I've seen too many people think that motivation and a great "conference weekend" feeling will give them what they need to have courage. The hard truth is that motivation is great, feelings are a gift from God, but motivation and our feelings were never supposed to be the determining factors of how we walk through life. Thank God for that, because feelings can fail us, and motivation takes more days off than any of us prefer. We must get to the root of lasting change and find the internal belief that will drive us forward - no matter how we feel or how many times we've failed. We must fight the good fight of faith and understand that it is a fight. Fights are hard and detrimental if you're not properly prepared. Think of this book like the montage in Rocky 4, before Rocky fights Ivan Drago. You are training with purpose in every repetition, every drop of sweat (physically, mentally, emotionally, and spiritually) for a fight that YOU CAN WIN if you're ready for it.

"Do you not know that in a race all the runners run, but only one gets the prize? Run in such a way as to get the prize. Everyone who competes in the games goes into strict training. They do it to get a crown that will not last, but we do it to get a crown that will last forever. Therefore I do not run like someone running aimlessly; I do not fight like a boxer beating the air. No, I strike a blow to my body and make it my slave so that after I have preached to others, I

myself will not be disqualified for the prize."
1 Corinthians 9:24-27 NIV

Too many people are living, or allowing dreams to live, in a mental or emotional prison cell that their doubts and failures have created; a prison that they have the power to bust through, but they choose to sit instead. Some people never experience the fullness of what God has in store for them. Hear me when I tell you I've found myself sitting in that cell more times than I want to admit; sitting there as the victim of life's circumstances and my failures. I have to make a choice, every time I find myself there: I must fight the good fight of faith for my life. I must choose to get back up one more time, to believe that God is good and that He is with me.

So here is what I want you to do. Set that friendly "shot-clock" and answer the question, "What dreams do you have that are sitting in that prison cell because of doubts and failures?"

I want to share an experience with you, and I pray it encourages you to step out of that cell, to break through the walls and experience the life of freedom Christ has called you to, because I almost left a dream in that cell...

When I first got saved, I believe the Lord put a passion in my heart to communicate to others about living in the fullness of what God has for their lives. I will never forget where I was when it happened, and how I encountered the Holy Spirit for the first time. I was 18 years old at Naval Air Station Pensacola, Florida. I got on my knees after a long weekend of partying over spring break in Panama City. I opened my Bible and asked God if He was real, if He could save me, and told Him that if this were true I would tell people about Him the rest of my life. The moments that followed changed my entire destiny; I felt the presence of God so strongly that every doubt was removed, every ounce of guilt was gone, and I was made completely new. I told one of my friends in the military that "God's presence is more satisfying than any high this world can offer." I experienced the reality of God, His goodness, and that you can truly taste and see that the Lord is good. It changed my life, and I wanted to tell everyone possible about it. I would dream about writing and speaking to share the beauty of God with people, to show that if God can meet me at my darkest place, He can meet anyone! His salvation doesn't depend on our works but His grace and it can set us free! But there were two major problems I ran into: I couldn't write and I was TERRIBLE at public speaking.

"Some people want it to happen, some wish it would happen, others make it happen."
Michael Jordan

My first time speaking publicly was unforgettable. I prepared for two weeks, I showed up and there were four students there. I spoke for an hour and fifteen minutes, confused everyone, and had two of them fall asleep. After speaking, I was humiliated. I left that place feeling like a failure and like I wanted to quit. I brought those feelings to the Lord, and then that night I felt the Lord tell me, "Just keep moving forward." I'll never forget it… So I did. I started to read books on public speaking, and took every opportunity that I could get. I was still terrible, but I was committed to fight for that dream. I was committed to work through my weaknesses and insecurities to see this dream become a reality, because on the other side of this dream in my heart were people's lives that I wanted to impact. I couldn't give up. I believe every dream God has given us is for the purpose of impacting the lives around us. Eventually, my talent caught up with my passions, and my dream became a reality. This is the fourth book that I've written, I've spoken on some massive stages, and I've seen hundreds of thousands of lives impacted because I fought for that dream. If God can do it for someone like me, He can do it with you! Just get back up! Keep moving forward and know if it's a dream you feel like God has given you, it's worth every drop of sweat to see it become a reality! It's worth the fight!

"It is never too late to be what you might have been."
George Eliot

As you're processing your dream or dreams, I want to share this final thought and story to help you move forward. I believe one of the greatest gifts we've been given is our imagination, and as Christians it's the fastest thing we hand over to the Kingdom of Darkness. We must put an end to that by thinking like athletes for King Jesus.

"Attitude is the 'little' thing that makes a big difference."
Winston Churchill

Coach Bob Stoops was one of my favorite coaches of all time in college football. I had the honor to meet him, speak to his team, and see his passion for Jesus above all else. One day I was with the team before they went out to play Texas Tech. My father and I were watching the game on the sidelines and had the opportunity to be with the team until they ran out on the field. Before the game, they had everyone leave the room who was not on the team or staff, but they let us stay, perhaps didn't see us in the corner. Coach started talking about the importance of watching game film, learning from mistakes, but then forgetting them. Focusing on the here and now and meditating on the past victories to bring future success. What happened next was incredible. The lights dimmed, and a hype video started playing. The music was on point and everything on that video was the team's successes from the week before. They wanted the team to only think on these things before they took the field. The video ended and the team sprinted out to the field. It was an amazing moment, and I'm happy to report they won that game. It set them on a course to make the first college football playoffs in their history.

"Summing it all up, friends, I'd say you'll do best by filling your minds and meditating on things true, noble, reputable, authentic, compelling, gracious—the best, not the worst; the beautiful, not the ugly; things to praise, not things to curse. Put into practice what you learned from me, what you heard and saw and realized. Do that, and God, who makes everything work together, will work you into his most excellent harmonies."
Philippians 4:8-9 MSG

So do this: learn from failure, but please never allow your failures to become doubts in what God can do through you. You are destined to live in freedom and to walk in extraordinarily courageous faith; you were not destined to spend your life sitting in the prison cell your doubts and fears have created.

"God can do anything, you know—far more than you could ever imagine or guess or request in your wildest dreams! He does it not by pushing us around but by working within us, his Spirit deeply and gently within us. Glory to God in the church! Glory to God in the Messiah, in Jesus! Glory down all the generations! Glory through all millennia! Oh, yes!"
Ephesians 3:20-21 MSG

Date

_____

Reflections

_____

_____

_____

_____

_____

_____

_____

_____

_____

_____

_____

_____

_____

_____

_____

_____

_____

_____

CHAPTER FOUR

Dealing with disappointment

"The righteous cry out, and the Lord hears them; he delivers them from all their troubles. The Lord is close to the brokenhearted and saves those who are crushed in spirit."
Psalms 34:17-18 NIV

A few days have passed, and the shepherd boy is still in total disbelief of his cowardice. Since that day he has been fighting through some very dark moments of depression. Until this point in his life, he always believed he had what it took to be a warrior. But the terror he felt in the face of the monster-like lion caused him to run from the fight he knows the heroes of old would have sprinted towards; that terror, and his actions of seeming cowardice, have made him question everything he is. Maybe he's just destined to be a "redheaded shepherd baby" that plays music to an audience of sheep.

As the shepherd is processing everything, another older shepherd comes running up to him.

"Have you heard?" the older shepherd says, panting for breath from his run and with excitement over the news.

"Heard what?" the young shepherd says, as he gets to his feet in curiosity.

"The great prophet Samuel is coming to your house. Rumor has it he is going to anoint the next king from your family! Some people say it's to sacrifice to the Lord and others think it's to honor Yahweh and anoint the next king. But either way, it's your house he is going to!"

All of a sudden, the passion and dreams of greatness come flooding into the shepherd's heart again; The thought of Yahweh sending a prophet to his home, the thought that maybe, just maybe, Yahweh has chosen him to be the next warrior king of Israel, gives him renewed strength.

The shepherd boy races down to the stream, strips off his clothes and dives in to clean up. As he is bathing his heart overflowing with joy and hope again, he sings to the Lord:

> *"The earth is the Lord's, and everything in it, the world, and all who live in it; for he founded it on the seas and established it on the waters. Who may ascend the mountain of the Lord? Who may stand in his holy place? The one who has clean hands and a pure heart, who does not trust in an idol or swear by a false god. They will receive blessing from the Lord and vindication from God their Savior. Such is the generation of those who seek him, who seek your face, God of Jacob. Lift up your heads, you gates; be lifted up, you ancient doors, that the King of glory may come in. Who is this King of glory? The Lord strong and mighty, the Lord mighty in battle. Lift up your heads, you gates; lift them up, you ancient doors, that the King of glory may come in. Who is he, this King of glory? The Lord Almighty— he is the King of glory."*
> *Psalms 24:1-10 NIV*

The shepherd finishes bathing and begins to prepare for the messenger to come notify him of their special guest. Any time a guest comes in to see the whole family, a messenger comes to notify the shepherd and then watch the sheep for a day or two. So now, the only thing to do is wait for the word. What a great day...

Every second seems like an hour waiting for this messenger. He practices slinging rocks at a precise target on a tree; he is now able to hit a hair on a tree from about 50 yards away while sprinting forward. His training is precise, and it helps him keep his mind off the time slowly ticking. Then it comes back to him, the weight of his recent failure: the memory of the sheep he was supposed to be protecting with his neck snapped by that monster-like lion while he hid in the tree like a coward. Tears fill the shepherd's eyes.

"Yahweh, forgive me. I was so scared, it felt like all my strength left me. I wanted to be strong and courageous like Joshua and Caleb, but I was terrified. Please see past my failure to my heart. I know I am not the biggest or the strongest, but I love you with all my heart. If you make me king I will live to bring glory to your name, and if you give me the strength of your Spirit I will destroy every enemy you have. Without your Spirit it is impossible for me to become a warrior, but with your Spirit I know I could scale any city wall, and I could certainly conquer every enemy you have. I could wipe the Philistines off the face of the earth!" As the shepherd finishes praying, he looks out at his flock as they eat, feeling a sense of Yahweh's peace in that moment, feeling like a sheep walking with the Lord, trusting Him fully, knowing come what may, this is the peace the shepherd lives for. He grabs his harp and begins to play one of his favorite songs from the greatest leader the Hebrew people have ever known...

"Lord, you have been our dwelling place in all generations. Before the mountains were brought forth, or ever you had formed the earth and the world, from everlasting to everlasting you are God. You return man to dust and say, "Return, O children of man!" For a thousand years in your sight are but as yesterday when it is past, or as a watch in the night. You sweep them away as with a flood; they are like a dream, like grass that is renewed in the morning: in the morning it flourishes and is renewed; in the evening it fades and withers. For we are brought to an end by your anger; by your wrath we are dismayed. You have set our iniquities before you, our secret sins in the light of your presence. For all our days pass away under your wrath; we bring our years to an end like a sigh. The years of our life are seventy, or even by reason of strength eighty; yet their span is but toil and trouble; they are soon gone, and we fly away. Who considers the power of your anger, and your wrath according to the fear of you? So teach us to number our days that we may get a heart of wisdom. Return, O Lord! How long? Have pity on your servants! Satisfy us in the morning with your steadfast love, that we may rejoice and be glad all our days. Make us glad for as many days as you have afflicted us, and for as many years as we have seen evil. Let your work be shown to your servants, and your glorious power

to their children. Let the favor of the Lord our God be upon us and establish the work of our hands upon us; yes, establish the work of our hands!"
Psalm 90:1-17 ESV

After finishing the song, the shepherd is lost in the moment, eyes closed and heart full as he is thinking of everything the Lord did for Moses and the Hebrew people. How God spoke to him, "Chazak Amats" and then that turned into the greatest war cry a warrior has ever known, **RAK CHAZAK!** A war cry that brings courage to any heart and fear to every enemy that hears it...

"RAK CHAZAK!" the shepherd boy yells at the top of his lungs, feeling his courage completely restored.
"RAK CHAZAK!" this time visualizing himself leading the Israelite people into battle.
"RAK CHAZAK!" one more time, thinking of destroying the race of people God hates, the Nephilim, the Giants that live and breathe to bring dishonor to the ways of Yahweh.

"If you give me the chance, Yahweh, I will destroy this race of people for your great name," the shepherd prays, completely forgetting how he just recently hid from a lion in fear.

This has always been one of his greatest strengths, living from his heart for Yahweh. Focusing on His power and not his ability...

Just then the old shepherd comes running over again, "What are you doing here?! Why aren't you there? Samuel is at your house now."

The shepherd's heart sinks, and tears fill his eyes. Overlooked again. Devastation fills his heart, courage gone, again.

"I guess... I guess... I wasn't invited." the shepherd barely gets out in response to the old shepherd.

The old shepherd, feeling awkward and unsure of what to do, slowly walks away to give the boy some space and time. "Sorry, buddy."

50

Once again, the shepherd is by himself with his sheep, weeping, knowing that without the touch of God, his destiny won't change. He will grow old like that shepherd that came by, and then die a lonely death. No woman wants to marry a shepherd, no man admires a shepherd, and no threat fears them.

The shepherd hears footsteps quickly approaching again, knowing it's not a threat, as the threats stalk so quietly you can barely hear them... Even if it was, death would be better than this...

"It's probably one of my brothers about to tell me they are going to be the next king," he says between his hands as he tries to wipe the tears away. The footsteps slow in frequency, and the shepherd takes a big breath to brace himself for the words that are about to be spoken to him...

"Samuel wants to see you..." the messenger says.

Chapter Four (b): Dealing with disappointment

"We must accept finite disappointment, but never lose infinite hope."
Martin Luther King, Jr.

Living with courage is an easy thing to talk about when you're sitting with a group of people around a fire, or when you're at a conference and you feel the motivation and inspiration of the moment; living with courage when you know the pain of failure, the humiliation of risking greatly and failing publicly, the feeling of despair when you're faced with disappointment that doesn't fit your theological understanding, is a different story.

Take a minute and go back to one of the most disappointing times in your life. Put yourself in that moment. Maybe it was a job interview that you thought you had in the bag. Maybe it was a person you thought you were going to marry. Maybe it was a person fighting a sickness that you thought the Lord would heal. Whatever it is, for us to be able to navigate through this properly and to empower us to live every day with the extraordinary courage we all need to accomplish our God-given dreams and passions, we must process through some of these disappointments. I know you're probably thinking, "Come on, let's get to the exciting part of this!" But too many people rush to the exciting part of living with their war cry, and they neglect the importance of a solid foundation. We need to fix the cracks so we can build a magnificently courageous, faith-filled life with a foundation that will not be destroyed!

"Disappointment is inevitable. But to become discouraged, there's a choice I make. God would never discourage me. He would always point me to himself to trust him. Therefore, my discouragement is from Satan. As you go through the emotions that we have, hostility is not from God, bitterness, unforgiveness, all of these are attacks from Satan."
Charles Stanley

The crack in a lot of our foundations is found in not mourning the disappointments we've experienced. We say things like, "toughen up and move on," or "you're too strong to let that get you down," or "you're too blessed to be stressed about this." And even though these can be very helpful things to say, they are not war cries if they aren't from a place of healing and wholeness. Trust me, because on this one, I am the chief of failures in this area. So, let's dive in…

Grab your pen, your timer and head to the journal page. You have 60 seconds to write down what comes to your mind when you think of the answer to this question:

What disappointment or disappointments do you have in your heart that you haven't brought before the Lord and mourned properly?

Take the time to write this down, meditate on it, and mourn; this is going to prepare your heart to face risk again from a place of healing and strength, not hurt and insecurity. Too many times in life we find ourselves trying to live courageously to cover up hurt and insecurities, hoping that the next major win will bring healing.

I recently experienced one of the most disappointing times of my professional career as an actor. My wife and I went all-in for films that we thought would inspire people across the world through gritty, raw stories from Old Testament warriors. We prayed, fasted, walked with the Spirit, and did our best to never get ahead of Him. We turned down money from people that had plans that did not honor our vision for the projects, and we had investors that believed in our projects to help us continue the journey. We felt courage and strength, and even though it was the hardest thing we have ever done, we felt like the Lord was leading us the entire time. We risked greatly, we gave God glory with every step and did our best to walk in integrity and honor the whole time. There were multiple moments I thought, with the amount of faith we were showing and the commitment to excellence by our entire team, there is no way the Lord would allow us to fail. Step by step we walked by faith, believing for breakthrough and power while facing insurmountable odds. I spent an entire year as an actor preparing to act as the most famous warrior in the Old Testament. An entire year saying no to other lead roles from other films to focus on this character. The fight choreography, the scene blocking, the unique mannerisms and nuances of the character, and memorizing the entire script as the lead. We were ready and expectant for God to show off. And then, everything failed. Pretty abruptly. Our team all had to move on, and it left me with a wound of disappointment so deep I didn't know how to process it. I cried out to the Lord, I cried again, and I cried some more. I fought through about three months of despair. Feeling like God abandoned me (I know He didn't). I felt alone, broken, and humiliated. Then I decided to move forward, without the knowledge of the importance of truly mourning this and bringing it to the Lord. Now hear me, there is a big difference in praying and pleading with the Lord to fix a situation, and praying to surrender your disappointment to Him, receive healing, and be content with never receiving an answer as to why everything happened; asking Him to heal you, trusting Him with your entire life moving forward, even though it feels like He failed you.

"Why am I discouraged? Why is my heart so sad? I will put my hope in God! I will praise him again— my Savior and my God!"
Psalm 42:5 NLT

I didn't have this realization until I was at a camp with some friends in the industry, where we had five days without our phones and time together and with the Lord. I sat one morning by a fire, a cup of coffee and tears in my eyes. I had a conversation with the Lord about my disappointment with everything my wife and I walked through, and that it impacted my trust for Him. I was doing what so many of us do: we get knocked down and then we get up and keep grinding forward. It's the American way, right? Pick yourself up by the bootstraps and keep moving. This is not the way of God's Kingdom. When we fall, we need to get back up, but we also need to receive healing from the Lord. We need to learn and study why we fell, and when we're healed, we get back into the fight. We have too many people on the battlefield of the faith that are bleeding out from the hurt of disappointment. And this is your charge: to take the time to heal, to sit with the Lord and bring your hurts to Him. To be honest, genuinely honest with Him. This doesn't have to be at a retreat; it can be in your kitchen tomorrow morning with your Bible and a cup of coffee. This can be on a walk tonight. This must be an intimate moment that is the start of a healing conversation.

When I brought this to the Lord, my healing happened. I spent time with Him and He comforted me in my pain of that disappointment. He didn't answer all my questions, but He did comfort me. And today, as I continue as an actor, author, and fitness influencer, I want to shout from the rooftops that I am healed from that hurt. God is so good.

"Have I not commanded you? Be strong and courageous. Do not be afraid; do not be discouraged, for the Lord your God will be with you wherever you go."
Joshua 1:9 NIV

I want to leave you with this before we move on to the next chapter; it's something that helped in my healing. When God allowed Satan to do everything he did to Job, God never told Job why He allowed it. God never (based on scripture) sat with Job and explained all of the events. I encourage you to read Job 38-42. God reveals his holiness and majesty to Job, and that brings the healing he needs. God didn't explain everything, but He restored Job.

"I know that you can do anything, and no one can stop you. You asked, 'Who is this that questions my wisdom with such ignorance?' It is I—and I was talking about things I knew nothing about, things far too wonderful for me. You said, 'Listen and I will speak! I have some questions for you, and you must answer them.' I had only heard about you before, but now I have seen you with my own eyes. I take back everything I said, and I sit in dust and ashes to show my repentance."
Job 42:2-6 NLT

So, no matter where you are in life, bring your disappointments to the Lord and be okay with not knowing why everything happened or didn't happen. Commit to trust Him and work from His peace and healing touch. If you do, extraordinary courage will become a habit in your life! Then you will be ready to start every day with the **RAK CHAZAK** mentality and truly understand the meaning behind it.

"Trust God from the bottom of your heart; don't try to figure out everything on your own. Listen for God's voice in everything you do, everywhere you go; he's the one who will keep you on track. Don't assume that you know it all. Run to God! Run from evil! Your body will glow with health, your very bones will vibrate with life! Honor God with everything you own; give him the first and the best. Your barns will burst, your wine vats will brim over. But don't, dear friend, resent God's discipline; don't sulk under his loving correction. It's the child he loves that God corrects; a father's delight is behind all this."
Proverbs 3:5-12 MSG

Date

_____

Reflections

_____

_____

_____

_____

_____

_____

_____

_____

_____

_____

_____

_____

_____

_____

_____

_____

CHAPTER FIVE

Experiencing breakthrough
power and moments

*"I waited patiently for the Lord; he inclined to me and heard my cry.
He drew me up from the pit of destruction, out of the miry bog, and
set my feet upon a rock, making my steps secure. He put a new
song in my mouth, a song of praise to our God. Many will see and
fear, and put their trust in the Lord."*
Psalm 40:1-3 ESV

The shepherd jumps to his feet and embraces the messenger so firmly
he picks him up off his feet. "Thank you!" the shepherd says with tears
of excitement in his eyes.

"You're welcome, but I have no idea what this is for; I was just told to
get you and watch the sheep until you return. Remember, Samuel is a
man of God to be feared; approach carefully and hurry to see him. He
is with your father and brothers, and will not let them sit down until you
get there," the messenger says with caution in his voice.

The shepherd grabs his things and begins to run as fast as he can
toward home, his heart overflowing with joy and excitement! As he is
running, he begins to shout this song of praise repeatedly, one of his
favorites:

*"The Lord is my shepherd; I shall not want. He makes me lie down
in green pastures. He leads me beside still waters. He restores my
soul. He leads me in paths of righteousness for his name's sake.
Even though I walk through the valley of the shadow of death, I will
fear no evil, for you are with me; your rod and your staff, they comfort
me. You prepare a table before me in the presence of my enemies;
you anoint my head with oil; my cup overflows. Surely goodness and
mercy shall follow me all the days of my life, and I shall dwell in the*

house of the Lord forever."
Psalm 23:1-6 ESV

Running on pure adrenaline and joy from the Lord, the shepherd sees his home in the distance. He pushes his run into a sprint. It feels like he can't get there fast enough, but then it hits him. What if that old shepherd was wrong? What if this isn't good news? What if…

The shepherd slows down and looks into his home. Everyone is standing up, like the messenger said, and in the middle is the great prophet, Samuel. Not even sure if he can make eye contact with him because of the rumors of his power from Yahweh, the shepherd looks down as he approaches the house. He keeps his head down and tries to slow his breathing.

As he takes a step into the house, everyone looks at him. The tension is heavy. The shepherd makes eye contact with each of his brothers as he walks in. Not angry, not full of revenge, but full of hurt and disappointment. Then he sees his father; they lock eyes. Unable to control himself, the young shepherd begins to weep. He could tell everyone was invited but him. His father again, overlooked him. A wound worse than any pain the physical body can experience…

Still not sure as to what is going on, the shepherd wipes the tears from his eyes, and does his best to keep his head low and his eyes down.

Suddenly, a voice breaks the silence; a voice more terrifying than any roar of a lion, that penetrates the shepherd's soul…

"David, Yahweh is proud of you. He has seen your heart and He has chosen you to be the king of Israel." These words from Samuel reach the souls of all in the room.

The great prophet grabs the horn of oil and approaches David. Feeling more terror than when the monster-like lion was staring at him, the strength of David's body fails him, and he falls to his knees.

The great prophet approaches him as David's body becomes

paralyzed with fear.

"On this day, in front of his father and brothers, I anoint David the son of Jesse to be the king of Israel," Samuel says as he reaches down to pour the oil.

As the oil hits David's head and runs down his body, he feels like he is going to die. The roar of a lion so loud it feels like his eardrums are going to explode, a surge of power so strong coursing through his veins it feels like his skin is going to melt, and his heart rate and breathing beyond his control. And then, total peace. Stillness and quiet.

"Rise, David son of Jesse, the Lord's anointed. Be strong and wait for the Lord to exalt you to king, in time. RAK CHAZAK David, RAK CHAZAK," Samuel says, and then embraces David with a hug that could heal any hurt. It is the first time in David's life he's felt a hug that feels straight from the heart of Yahweh.

Samuel then turns, walks toward the door without saying another word, and then exits, leaving David standing there awkwardly in the middle of the room. David looks across the room at his father and brothers, this time a different person. Full of the Spirit of Yahweh and His power. This is no longer the "redheaded shepherd baby," but the future king of Israel. Nobody says a word. David gives a slight smile, grabs a loaf of bread from the table, and heads back out to the field to be with his sheep.

"The Lord said to Samuel, "How long will you grieve over Saul, since I have rejected him from being king over Israel? Fill your horn with oil, and go. I will send you to Jesse the Bethlehemite, for I have provided for myself a king among his sons." And Samuel said, "How can I go? If Saul hears it, he will kill me." And the Lord said, "Take a heifer with you and say, 'I have come to sacrifice to the Lord.' And invite Jesse to the sacrifice, and I will show you what you shall do. And you shall anoint for me him whom I declare to you." Samuel did what the Lord commanded and came to Bethlehem. The elders of the city came to meet him trembling and said, "Do you come

peaceably?" And he said, "Peaceably; I have come to sacrifice to the Lord. Consecrate yourselves, and come with me to the sacrifice." And he consecrated Jesse and his sons and invited them to the sacrifice. When they came, he looked on Eliab and thought, "Surely the Lord's anointed is before him." But the Lord said to Samuel, "Do not look on his appearance or on the height of his stature, because I have rejected him. For the Lord sees not as man sees: man looks on the outward appearance, but the Lord looks on the heart." Then Jesse called Abinadab and made him pass before Samuel. And he said, "Neither has the Lord chosen this one." Then Jesse made Shammah pass by. And he said, "Neither has the Lord chosen this one." And Jesse made seven of his sons pass before Samuel. And Samuel said to Jesse, "The Lord has not chosen these." Then Samuel said to Jesse, "Are all your sons here?" And he said, "There remains yet the youngest, but behold, he is keeping the sheep." And Samuel said to Jesse, "Send and get him, for we will not sit down till he comes here." And he sent and brought him in. Now he was ruddy and had beautiful eyes and was handsome. And the Lord said, "Arise, anoint him, for this is he." Then Samuel took the horn of oil and anointed him in the midst of his brothers. And the Spirit of the Lord rushed upon David from that day forward. And Samuel rose up and went to Ramah."
1 Samuel 16:1-13 ESV

Chapter Five (b): Experiencing breakthrough power and moments

"I will study. I will prepare. And one day my chance will come."
Abraham Lincoln

These moments, the moments of affirmation from the Lord, are worth all the blood, sweat, and tears we poured out in the valley of the shadow of death. Those dark stretches of time when we feel alone and forgotten, but we chose to endure; those moments when we thought the Enemy had us surrounded, outnumbered, and defeated, but we trusted the Lord and kept moving forward no matter how it looked. I believe those moments are more valuable to our character and faith than anything this world has to offer, and our job is to experience them fully and never forget them. This part of the book was a joy for me to write, thinking about how this moment with David could have been, and it could impact all our lives.

Our past, our family, and what others say about us does not define our destiny; God's favor does. I've heard many speakers say that one touch of God's favor is worth more than a lifetime of labor. Reminding my soul of how God's favor can change everything in a moment helps me persevere when it feels like I've been overlooked. Knowing that God is looking for hearts fully committed to Him to use mightily, not people who have the perfect family, friends and résumés. Thank God...

"The eyes of the Lord search the whole earth in order to strengthen those whose hearts are fully committed to Him."
2 Chronicles 16:9a NLT

Our world refers to situations of breakthrough as luck, but as believers in Jesus Christ we know it's God's timing intersecting with our preparation. I want to share a personal story I've never shared in writing to help illuminate this even more, because I believe reading this book is not a mistake, or just chance; I believe it's a time in your life ordained by God. I believe God has something so great in store for you that your mind would be intimidated if you saw the whole plan unfold. I believe He is working that out as you read this, and I believe a very crucial ingredient to living out this destiny God has for you is how committed you will be to the process of preparation, perspiration, and worship, while you wait to see the Lord's breakthrough power in your life.

"Do you not know? Have you not heard? The Lord is the everlasting God, the Creator of the ends of the earth. He will not grow tired or weary, and his understanding no one can fathom. He gives strength to the weary and increases the power of the weak. Even youths grow tired and weary, and young men stumble and fall; but those who hope in the Lord will renew their strength. They will soar on wings like eagles; they will run and not grow weary, they will walk and not be faint."
Isaiah 40:28-31 NIV

The process of writing Soulcon Challenge took five and a half years. It was an endurance race, and there were hundreds of times I was tempted to quit. There were well-meaning people in my life trying to talk me out of "wasting my time" writing a book, and do something that will build financial stability. And then there were people who were mean and would gossip. It hurt, but the choice to drink from the poison of offense and listen to their negative talk, or ignore it entirely, was up to me. Being hurt is inevitable in life if you are trying to do anything worthwhile for the King of kings, but taking offense is a poison we must choose not to drink. I decided to charge forward, and along the way had publishers that wanted to work with me only if I made the book for men and women; I knew that book was supposed to be for men. I turned down every opportunity and decided to self-publish it; a very risky, often foolish move, but compromising on the heart of the book for sales would be riskier. I wanted to honor God with every step, and make sure my motives were not driven by making money from sales, because the wealth He might bring is the only wealth we should truly want. The hard work is up to us, and the outcome is up to God. This is easy to write, but tough to trust as life plays out...

I will never forget when the day of the book release was approaching; I was so stoked I couldn't stand it. All of that hard work was about to pay off. I couldn't wait to see men's lives impacted by this book in the way that mine was. As an author, I knew how massive the launch day was: publishers are watching, people are watching, and it's a day that really forecasts the success of the life of the book. I prayed, prepped, prayed, fasted, and prayed some more. I left no stone unturned. I did everything I knew to have a potentially viral launch day. Then, the day finally came…

It was devastating, embarrassing, and the day I almost completely gave up. The launch day finished and I had sold 17 copies of Soulcon Challenge; a crushing defeat. That would be like David running up against Goliath, getting spanked over Goliath's knee, then getting sent back, without even the honor of death. It felt like that day would define my career moving forward. People would always view me as the warrior that thought he could slay giants but got sent back home to shepherd his dad's sheep.

I cried going to bed that night. I wanted to quit everything. When I woke up the next morning, I still felt every emotion, just with a rested body. I walked into my living room, grabbed a cup of coffee and my Bible, and I felt the Lord tell me to "just keep moving forward." I said, "yes Sir," and I did just that. In the face of public defeat, I got back up and moved forward one day at a time. And I wish I could say everything changed that next day, but it didn't. It seemed like every day was a year, and every question from people in my life of, "how did your book launch go?" was an arrow to my soul. But I answered the questions honestly, and I was also honest with myself. It was hard, but I believed the message in the book was important, so I pressed on. I started speaking to men everywhere I could. Groups of 5-40 were the average. Then, one day, I was invited to be the keynote speaker at a men's conference expecting 3,500 attendees…

I already had the scars of public defeat with my book launch, and to that point I had barely sold 250 copies in about 5 months, but I accepted the invitation to speak and again risked greatly for the Lord, and the passion I believe He put on my heart.

What I did next was extraordinary in the best way… I felt in prayer that I was supposed to plan for breakthrough at this conference. Most of the time when I spoke I would sell about 10-15 copies of my book. But I felt like I was supposed to prepare and be ready for more. I spent the last of my money, about $12,000 on books and merchandise for this conference. Everything I had.

I was at the conference, and it was time. I will never forget being backstage. Everything on the line, and on top of that, I had the worst case of strep leading up to this; a fever I couldn't break and sleepless nights. I was completely exhausted. I got on my knees before I walked out in front of those men and I asked the Lord for strength, for him to speak through me. Then, for the first time in my life, I felt what I believe David felt on that day of anointing. My sickness left my body, my strength was back stronger than ever, and I felt God's power bursting out of my veins. I walked on the stage, and everything changed...

Men's lives were impacted greatly, every single piece of my merchandise sold out, and parts of that video went viral, sending my book sales to a level that helped me step into speaking and traveling as my full-time career. From that point forward, my book was translated into 3 different languages and started a movement in men's hearts around the country and in different parts of the world. I will never forget what it took to get there, though: risk, endurance, pressing through the hardest and loneliest nights, and committing to honor God no matter the outcome. I write this to inspire your soul to extraordinary courage in your everyday life. If God did it for me then, I promise He can do it for you now.

Extraordinary courage in our lives is possible if it's preceded by extraordinary intimacy with the Lord.

The final thing is one that brings tears to my eyes. I want every person to be impacted hearing this: the anointing God has for you depends on your heart, not your physical appearance. We live in a "perfect filter" and "social media status" driven world, and that is NOT how God's Kingdom works. God sees your heart, and has already measured your destiny based on how He has gifted and equipped you. Never spend another second thinking that because you look a certain way, it's going to limit your destiny; that's what Jesse thought about David, and boy was he wrong. Your destiny in God's Kingdom comes down to your faith and the actions that follow. It's simple, but we can never forget the greatest battles in our lives are to live consistently, with passion and a commitment to excellence.

"For as the body apart from the spirit is dead, so also faith apart from works is dead."
James 2:26 ESV

That's why knowing this war cry is so critical in your life. Knowing God loves you, God believes in you, and God is for you will give you the confidence to rest, and know victory is your banner. I believe God is looking at you today saying, "RAK CHAZAK, (YOUR FIRST NAME.) RAK CHAZAK."

From this day forward, I want you to write this on your bathroom mirror with a marker, or with a sticky note: "RAK CHAZAK, (YOUR FIRST NAME.) RAK CHAZAK." Say this out loud before every day begins, and before it ends. Say it knowing God sees greatness in you. Say it reminding your soul that YOU have what it takes if you continue to walk in the Spirit and not the flesh.

Love you guys! **RAK CHAZAK!**

"Be strong and very courageous. Be careful to obey all the instructions Moses gave you. Do not deviate from them, turning either to the right or to the left. Then you will be successful in everything you do. Study this Book of Instruction continually. Meditate on it day and night so you will be sure to obey everything written in it. Only then will you prosper and succeed in all you do. This is my command—be strong and courageous! Do not be afraid or discouraged. For the Lord your God is with you wherever you go."
Joshua 1:7-9 NLT

Date

_____

Reflections

CHAPTER SIX

Fighting
from victory

*"I believe that I shall look upon the goodness of the Lord in the land
of the living! Wait for the Lord; be strong, and let your heart take
courage; wait for the Lord!"*
Psalm 27:13-14 ESV

A few months have passed since that day that changed everything in David's life. That day where God's spirit rushed upon him with ferocity as Samuel anointed him the next king of Israel, in front of the ones who never believed in him: his brothers and his father. One thing they didn't know, is what David experienced in that moment; the moment where every fiber of his being became a warrior. When Samuel said "RAK CHAZAK, David. RAK CHAZAK," David knew he was a different person. That war cry was no longer a cry to be someone great, but a statement to the heart of a warrior, a piece of communication affirming everything David had hoped for. It was, for the first time, knowledge that victory was going to be the outcome of every challenge ahead. RAK CHAZAK has a different meaning now. It's speaking victory that has already been won, speaking strength and courage that is already there, rather than the hope of courage in the face of battle. RAK CHAZAK is now a mentality of strength, and victory, because Yahweh is with David. RAK CHAZAK is a war cry that turned into a lifestyle in the heart of this shepherd, this warrior, this future king.

It's now almost spring in Israel. It's that time of year where the hope for a warmer tomorrow impacts everyone's attitude for the better, but the nights still bring the bone chilling despair of winter. Nobody enjoys it, no matter how much they pretend, except for one young man...

David always ends these bitter cold days with a fire and a few songs for his sheep, the captive audience he's grown to love. Ever since his anointing, nothing can steal his joy. He has grown to appreciate every season, knowing Yahweh saw him and chose him even when others overlooked him. This song is an overflow of his love and gratitude for Yahweh, and one of his new favorites:

"O Lord, our Lord, how majestic is your name in all the earth! You have set your glory above the heavens. Out of the mouth of babies and infants, you have established strength because of your foes, to still the enemy and the avenger. When I look at your heavens, the work of your fingers, the moon and the stars, which you have set in place, what is man that you are mindful of him, and the son of man that you care for him? Yet you have made him a little lower than the heavenly beings and crowned him with glory and honor. You have given him dominion over the works of your hands; you have put all things under his feet, all sheep and oxen, and also the beasts of the field, the birds of the heavens, and the fish of the sea, whatever passes along the paths of the seas. O Lord, our Lord, how majestic is your name in all the earth!"
Psalm 8:1-9 ESV

David finishes the song in deep wonder, looking up at the stars, tears in his eyes and a heart full of gratitude. He sets his harp to the side and leans in toward the fire to warm his hands. Every time he sees the flames, he thinks of Moses encountering Yahweh at the bush that was burning but never consumed: Moses, thinking his failure had defined his destiny, just like David had when he was overlooked his whole life. Moses listened, obeyed, and shifted the course of the Hebrew people through his obedience.

"I wonder if he ever felt this power, this unstoppable force coursing through his veins, longing for a battle…" David said quietly to himself. The majority of David's thought life was spent meditating on the warriors throughout the history of the Hebrews. Moses, Caleb, and Joshua were some of his favorites.

Suddenly, one of David's sheep gets to his feet and approaches. David's gaze pierces through the fire, knowing in his heart what it is; He smiles like a Leviathan from old about to devour a fatted calf. No more fear, no terror, no cowardice; this is a completely different man: a warrior anointed by the hand of Yahweh, longing for the taste of justice, full of hope that this is the adversary he has been waiting for... the half-demon, half-lion.

He steadies his breath, pulls a stone from his pouch, and drops his sling to his side, all the while not breaking eye contact with the line of brush across from the fire.

A few more of his sheep pop to their feet and walk toward David. He remains still, hunting, waiting, no longer the prey. It feels like fire is burning in his veins as he waits to release the stone on whatever is in the brush. He knows it's a threat because he still hasn't heard it. He sees the brush move and his eyes lock in on the location. Joy fills his heart so much he wants to sing, but instead remains still and quiet. Waiting...

The creature slowly steps out of the brush. With the bitter cold, every breath from its mouth looks like smoke coming out of a Leviathan. It's clear this lion wants one thing: David's flesh and blood. The lion stares at David just like before, but this time, it's not a shepherd boy looking back at him.

They make eye contact, neither one taking the time to blink.

"RAK CHAZAK," David says, as if he is speaking victory into the ear of the lion.

A deep, low growl escapes the lion's mouth as if answering back. It takes a step forward and David doesn't wait one second longer...

His sling whips over his head so fast the lion doesn't even have time to blink; the stone releases, hurling through the air, and crushes the left eye of the lion. Blood splatters all over his mane and he lets out a loud roar of pain as he steps back, last step that lion will ever take...

David leaps over the fire and sprints toward the lion with the speed of Yahweh. By the time the lion balances himself, David crashes into him, grabbing his blood-soaked mane and flipping the beast over on its back. David turns the head of the lion to the side so he can make eye contact and savors this moment; he sees fear in the creature's eye for the first time. David screams "RAK!!!" and strikes the lion so hard in his right eye that his skull caves in from the blow… "CHAZAK…" David exhales as he releases the corpse of the lion.

Typically the warrior would cut the head of their opponent off and put it in a special place to remind them of the victory. With this one there was no head remaining. David snaps off one of his front teeth and puts it in his pouch.

David stands up, longing for something else to be out there, for battle to continue. With the anointing from Yahweh he feels as if he can destroy every single one of the threats to the Israelite people. "Some day…" he says to himself.

He grabs the massive beast by the legs and throws him into the fire with one swing. David walks back over to where he was sitting and watches the hideous beast burn.

"Yahweh, if you give me the chance, I will hunt every single one of the Philistines down just like this. I will lead the Israelite men into every battle to eliminate the Philistine bloodline for your great name."

Chapter Six (b): Fighting from victory

What would your life look like if you were the predator to every challenge and not the prey? What if, when a challenge bursts out of the brush, you were ready and confident of victory? Well, here's the great news… You can be! If you set up the principals and philosophy of this war cry in your everyday life, you will have this level of extraordinary courage as well.

I want you to consider how you steward your body. This is a battlefield on which too many people are ceding victory. The stewardship of our bodies matters, because it was bought with the price of Jesus' blood on the cross. As believers in Jesus Christ, it is our choice to honor him or dishonor him with our bodies. Grab the timer, set the "shot-clock," and be completely honest with yourself as you answer this question, just a yes or no answer:

Are you living victoriously with full control of your body on a daily basis?

"Or do you not know that your body is a temple of the Holy Spirit within you, whom you have from God? You are not your own, for you were bought with a price. So glorify God in your body."
1 Corinthians 6:19-20 ESV

This chapter is going to pour even more courage into your soul to steward your body with excellence. I believe this is at the heart of breaking any addiction, any bad habit or mindset of ignorance, that we think is leading to bliss but deep down is leading to destruction.

There is no temptation in this world that has the power to overcome the strength of Christ in you. Nothing. No porn addiction, no sugar addiction, no drug addiction, no alcohol addiction, no gambling addiction… NO TEMPTATION has more power than the power of Christ in you. You have what it takes because Christ lives in you.

"You, dear children, are from God and have overcome them, because the one who is in you is greater than the one who is in the world."
1 John 4:4 NIV

Let's take three very practical areas and put our war cry into practice, with the hopes that this builds a habit of extraordinary courage with every single challenge we face. I believe it will...

The first area is with your diet. Most of us eat 2-4 times a day and have some snacks here and there. People ask me frequently, "What's your favorite diet plan?" My answer is always the same: "The one that fuels the best version of you every day." The best version of you is the person walking in the Spirit and having the fruits of the Spirit manifesting in every area of your life. If you struggle with self-control, no diet or exercise program can fix it. As a believer, that can only be fixed by intimacy with the Spirit; when that happens, we will have the fruit of every attribute He has, and that fuels the best version of ourselves. Do yourself a favor: from this day forward, view food this way.

Food is a gift from God. Food is created to fuel with, to feast with, and to fast from, but it is never created to be the master of our soul. That is called gluttony, and God hates gluttony because of the destruction it causes in the lives of His children.

You are created to walk in victory over appetites of your flesh. You have what it takes to be like David, sitting around that fire ready to conquer that lion, but maybe that lion is your lust for sugar and carbs. You have what it takes to never spend one more second of your life feeling out of control with regards to food. Now, will that be easy? Not at all. But food can become a servant to your lifestyle and empower you to accomplish the dreams the Lord has placed on your heart. Praise God. Starting today, before every meal, speak your war cry before you eat: RAK CHAZAK. Never forget that one of the Godliest things we can do is feast with our loved ones. Don't be afraid of food. Be in control and enjoy it! I believe a healthy diet without feasting is like a marriage without sex. Feast, fuel, fast but never surrender the control of your will to food; that is gluttony.

"Excellence is achieved by the mastery of the fundamentals."
Vince Lombardi

The second area involves the use of your smart phone. I believe one of the greatest tactics of the Enemy in our lives today is distracting us to discourage us from proper preparation with the goal of our missing out on opportunities. I don't believe in luck, but I do believe opportunities are missed when we become distracted and lazy. I want you to be found ready when every God opportunity comes your way. Just like we talked about food serving the purpose of your life, your smart phone should serve the same purpose. So here is a tactic: before you open your smart phone, say RAK CHAZAK. Remind your soul not to lose control, but to use your phone as the tool it was created to be.

However your devices are destroying your soul - with the viewing of pornography, maybe talking to people you shouldn't, feeding a lack of contentment, covetousness and or pride, these are just a few examples, please pursue accountability. Confess to a trusted friend, as we did in the self-inflicted wound section, and get help. I want to shout this on the rooftops and right into your soul: the war for purity is a winnable war in Christ, and we must win it daily! We can conquer lust and throw it into the fire as David threw the lion. The choice is ours; the power is Christ's. It's a winnable war! Future generations depend on our walking in this extraordinary courage with the purity of our heart, as much as in any other area of our life. Commit with me to win this battle; in Christ, you have what it takes!

"Therefore, since we are surrounded by such a great cloud of witnesses, let us throw off everything that hinders and the sin that so easily entangles. And let us run with perseverance the race marked out for us, fixing our eyes on Jesus, the pioneer and perfecter of faith. For the joy set before him he endured the cross, scorning its shame, and sat down at the right hand of the throne of God."
Hebrews 12:1-2 NIV

The final area is with your physical fitness. I could write an entire book on all the areas in which we could put this into practice, but I want to share a few that I believe will become habit-drivers in every area of our lives. I see too many people shortcutting their workouts because they are so distracted on their phones. I want you to commit to change that. I want your physical fitness to reflect the internal belief that your life has magnificent purpose and value, that your dreams are worth fighting for, that your body being in optimal shape isn't optional for the amazing plan God has for your life, and that you will not waste time at any point of your life, especially at the gym. Before you walk into the gym, visualize some of the great warriors in the Bible: Abraham, Moses, Caleb, Joshua, David, Samson, etc. Picture them watching your workout, cheering you on to become the best version of yourself. As you walk into the gym, say RAK CHAZAK before you enter that battlefield of fitness. Your body will fight for the path of least resistance and ease, and you must bring it into subjection during that time. I have this mentality that I want to share:

I will drown my doubts in sweat with physical exertion so I can pursue my dreams with total immersion.

In conclusion, you are not the prey of any challenge, temptation, or addiction! You are more than a conqueror in Christ Jesus; greater is He that is in you than he who is in this world! From this day forward, view every challenge like David did sitting at the campfire, longing to have victory in the battle about to begin! **RAK CHAZAK!**

"Don't you realize that in a race everyone runs, but only one person gets the prize? So run to win! All athletes are disciplined in their training. They do it to win a prize that will fade away, but we do it for an eternal prize. So I run with purpose in every step. I am not just shadowboxing. I discipline my body like an athlete, training it to do what it should. Otherwise, I fear that after preaching to others I myself might be disqualified."
1 Corinthians 9:24-27 NLT

Date

Reflections

CHAPTER SEVEN

Serving with humility and honor in every season

"Blessed be the Lord, my rock, who trains my hands for war, and my fingers for battle; he is my steadfast love and my fortress, my stronghold and my deliverer, my shield and he in whom I take refuge, who subdues peoples under me."
Psalm 144:1-2 ESV

The weather is still biting cold, the winter dragging on with no end in sight; this hasn't bothered David, however. He has the tooth of the beast in his pouch and a new hide to keep him warm: the skin of a bear who tried to take one of his sheep away and met the same fate as the lion. He enjoys wearing the hide while he sings praises to Yahweh around the fire in the evenings.

David reaches to grab his harp and begins to worship, finding that as he waits for Yahweh's timing for his transition to warrior-king, he loves to worship more than ever. Just as his fingers and hands feel anointed for battle, he feels his voice has that same strength. David leans back, the bear's head as his hood, he smiles and begins to sing:

"The earth is the Lord's and the fullness thereof, the world and those who dwell therein, for he has founded it upon the seas and established it upon the rivers. Who shall ascend the hill of the Lord? And who shall stand in his holy place? He who has clean hands and a pure heart, who does not lift up his soul to what is false and does not swear deceitfully. He will receive blessing from the Lord and righteousness from the God of his salvation. Such is the generation of those who seek him, who seek the face of the God of Jacob. Selah Lift up your heads, O gates! And be lifted up, O ancient doors, that the King of glory may come in. Who is this King of glory? The Lord, strong and mighty, the Lord, mighty in battle! Lift up your

*heads, O gates! And lift them up, O ancient doors, that the King of
glory may come in. Who is this King of glory? The Lord of hosts, he
is the King of glory! Selah"*
Psalm 24:1-10 ESV

Finishing the song, David begins to visualize what it must have been like to be standing with the Israelites when the walls of Jericho crashed down. People have shared the stories for generations, what their family members saw and experienced, the awe and fear of Yahweh that must have consumed them as they heard and watched the walls of the largest city crash down.

*"But Joshua commanded the people, 'You shall not shout [the battle
cry] nor let your voice be heard nor let a word come out of your
mouth, until the day I tell you to shout. Then you shall shout!'"*
Joshua 6:10 AMP

Then, after not speaking for almost seven days, you hear it: the trumpets blast, the entire Israelite nation shouts the war cry that brings terror to everyone that hears it…

"RAK CHAZAK!"

The war cry that is confident of victory by the hand of Yahweh himself; a war cry that David finally understands.

*"So the people shouted, and the trumpets were blown. As soon as
the people heard the sound of the trumpet, the people shouted a
great shout, and the wall fell down flat, so that the people went up
into the city, every man straight before him, and they captured the
city."*
Joshua 6:20 ESV

Some people have said, though maybe just exaggerated rumors, that every one of the leaders of the 31 kingdoms in the promised land heard the war cry that day, instilling fear in each one.

"If only I can lead people half as well as the great warlords Caleb and Joshua, my life would be an accomplishment as king," David says to himself while deep in thought. Then a voice breaks the silence around him:

"Son, you're needed on the battlefield," Jesse says, as David's heart leaps in his chest.

"Thank you, Father! I am more than ready!" David says, ready to bring God's justice on the Philistines.

Jesse said to his son David, "Take this ephah of roasted grain and these ten loaves of bread for your brothers and hurry to their camp. Take along these ten cheeses to the commander of their unit. See how your brothers are and bring back some assurance from them. They are with Saul and all the men of Israel in the Valley of Elah, fighting against the Philistines." 1 Samuel 17:17-19 NIV)

David's heart sinks. Every emotion from his childhood comes rushing back to him: being overlooked, the outcast of the family, and misunderstood.

"Yes, sir," David says but he wants to plead his case. He wants to share with Jesse what happened when he was anointed, the power and strength that came over him. Not only is he anointed king, but he is anointed as a warrior. He wants to tell him about the lion and the bear, but he knows he would be wasting his breath. Yahweh commands to honor father and mother, so David chooses honor.

"It's a long travel day, so make sure to wake up early and get started. I will send a shepherd to you to watch the flock while you're gone. And David…"

"Yes Father…"

"Stop wasting our money on things like that bear hide. Only men who are brave enough and strong enough to kill a bear should wear those. Do not wear that tomorrow. You really need to grow up and stop pretending like you're a warrior. But tomorrow you have a chance to serve the true warriors of the family and this nation. Serve them well and do not get in their way."

Chapter Seven (b): Serving with humility and honor in every season

I want to share again that the war cry that is confident of victory by the hand of Yahweh himself; is a war cry that David finally understands. I share it again because I believe today is the day where you become fully aware of the strength, courage, and victory you have in Christ. I believe there is an awakening that can happen in your life where you know (not just think) in the core of your being that victory has already been won; victory over your addictions, your lusts, your apathy, or any area of your life that isn't growing to look more like Jesus every day. I believe the Lord can pour revelation knowledge into you right now: that YOU HAVE WHAT IT TAKES TO WIN because the Spirit of God lives in you. You have His strength, His courage, and the victory He won on the cross in you, every single day! You don't have to walk in fear any longer; you can walk in power and knowledge that you have what it takes to be successful because you're walking in Christ. Porn has lost its grip in Jesus' Name! Drugs have lost their grip in Jesus' Name! Gambling, gluttony, jealously and any fear has lost its grip on your soul in the powerful name of Jesus! You are free because of Jesus! Walk, live, eat, sleep, train, breathe, and do everything like the warrior you are! I hope and pray you receive that, and never forget it…

"Let the words of my mouth, and the meditation of my heart, be acceptable in thy sight, O LORD, my strength, and my redeemer."
Psalm 19:14 KJV

Before writing this chapter, I have never thought of David sitting there with the hide of the bear he killed draped over him keeping him warm, his harp in his hands, singing praise to the Lord. The moment that visual entered my imagination it shifted my thinking and convicted me deeply. I want my life to look like this part of the book with David. No matter who looks into my life at any point, no matter how hopeless a situation looks, I want to be sitting there with a strong attitude in the midst of it all, clothed in victory and singing praises to the King of kings. I want that with all of my heart, but I don't have it yet. I feel overwhelmed by how frequently I can clothe myself with self-pity, and sit and sulk in my selfishness; how, in those moments, I will go work out and listen to the loudest rap or rock music possible to numb myself from the pain. I justify it by saying it's my therapy time, but honest reflection reveals it is my attempt to hide. This is not the best for my life, and I want the best because I know my actions inspire my loved ones around me. Whether I want them to or not, my kids will follow my actions more than my words. I am going to share the three specific areas in which the Lord convicted my heart from this visual, and since this conviction came while writing this book, it's possible that this might be for strength, courage and conviction in your soul as well.

"The eyes of the Lord search the whole earth in order to strengthen those whose hearts are fully committed to him.
2 Chronicles 16:9a NLT

The first area is with the words we speak, and the question rang in my soul, "If the words you speak throughout the day were your clothing would you be clothed in victory or in defeat?" I want so badly to have my words be like this bear hide around David's body, clothing me in victory and protecting me from the elements around me, but I have some work to do. Too many times I allow idle words of defeat, self-pity, or just stupidity to come out of my mouth. There are times with my family when my words are sarcastic, harsh, and short. From this day forward, I commit to make my words reflect the war cry of my heart. I don't want to just say RAK CHAZAK; I want to live it and believe it. So here is where I'm starting: I have put the following paragraph together, printed it out, and committed to speak it before I read my Bible and before I eat every meal. I want to train my mind to hear words of victory from my lips, and train my tongue to speak victory. I would encourage you to do the same:

I am strong in the Lord. I am full of energy. I can do all things through Christ Who strengthens me. I am valuable, talented, and because of Jesus I have a bright future. In Christ, my strength is being renewed day by day. This is the day the Lord has made; I will rejoice and be glad in it! Today is going to be a great day!

In the Name of Jesus, I declare from this day forward that I see myself the way God sees me. I am highly favored. I am crowned

with glory and honor. I am the righteousness of God in Christ Jesus.

In Jesus' Name, every morning when I wake up, I will speak and expect God's favor to go before me and surround me as a shield. I declare in Jesus' Name that doors are now open for me that people have said are impossible to open. I believe that God is with me, that He is for me, and that in Christ I am more than a conqueror.

Amen.

The next area is with the words we hear. When I visualized David sitting there, I knew the pinpoint of conviction for me: the words I listen to during my workouts. How can I say that I'm a man after God's heart if I'm listening to songs full of words that break the Lord's heart? Conviction set in deeply here, and anytime we feel conviction we have a choice. Humble ourselves and repent, or harden our hearts by making excuses and justifying our actions. As believers, we know one choice leads to honor from the Lord and one choice leads to destruction. I always want to be found making the choice of humility and repentance; today I commit to you, if you ever see me in a gym you can come up to me and do a music check for accountability. My music will be honoring to the Lord.

The final area is with the attitude we keep. Visualizing David sitting there, clothed in victory and making the decision to sing praises to the Lord, then being humble enough to not talk back to his father really convicted me. There are so many times in my life where I act humble on the outside, but my heart is demanding respect; we know that out of the abundance of our heart, our mouth speaks (Luke 6:45). This area alone could be an entire relationship book, and even though I won't deep-dive into this, I can't help but think how much my relationships will be impacted by my having a constant attitude of victory and confidence in Christ, and a humble heart that doesn't have to demand respect from anyone; just like David did in this chapter. He held his tongue and he acted in honor. That led David to the greatest moment of honor in his life.

"Before destruction a man's heart is haughty, but humility comes before honor."
Proverbs 18:12 ESV

I hope we all choose to allow these areas of conviction, or any other areas of conviction that are personal to you, to impact our souls, to repent if needed, and always find ourselves on the road of honor and humility with the Lord, because it's only on that road that we find ourselves honored and elevated by the King of kings and Lord of lords. Only on that road does the Goliath in our story find an unbeatable opponent…

"You save a humble people, but your eyes are on the haughty to bring them down. For you are my lamp, O Lord, and my God lightens my darkness. For by you I can run against a troop, and by my God I can leap over a wall. This God—his way is perfect; the word of the Lord proves true; he is a shield for all those who take refuge in him. "For who is God, but the Lord? And who is a rock, except our God? This God is my strong refuge and has made my way blameless. He made my feet like the feet of a deer and set me secure on the heights. He trains my hands for war, so that my arms can bend a bow of bronze. You have given me the shield of your salvation, and your gentleness made me great."
2 Samuel 22:28-36 ESV

Date

_____

Reflections

_____

_____

_____

_____

_____

_____

_____

_____

_____

_____

_____

_____

_____

_____

_____

_____

_____

_____

CHAPTER EIGHT

Courage and confidence in chaos

"Early in the morning David left the flock in the care of a shepherd, loaded up and set out, as Jesse had directed. He reached the camp as the army was going out to its battle positions, shouting the war cry."
1 Samuel 17:20 NIV

After the long walk with the supplies, David sees it, the thing he's dreamed about for his entire life: the battle positions. He takes a deep breath, savoring the moment, dreaming of the day he is king and present with his men for every battle. He knows the battlefield will be his destiny, and feels that it will always be the safest place for him.

Then, he hears it: the roar of the most terrifying war cry the world has ever known...

"RAK CHAZAK!" the army shouts in one accord, sounding like a lion ready to devour.

But something odd happens that catches David off guard. The Israelites don't sprint into battle; they stand still and wait for the battle lines to be drawn.

"This isn't how we fight…" David says to himself in utter confusion. He grabs the handles of the cart he is pulling and continues down the hill to try to figure out what is going on.

Getting to the base of the valley, David leaves the cart of food with the keeper of the supplies and heads out to see his brothers. Walking through the line of warriors, he notices urine falling from some of their legs. The smell is horrendous. They are terrified.

"Abinidab! Hey! How are you?" David says, to get his brother's attention.

"What are you doing here, David? This isn't the place for a shepherd… I don't know if this is even a place for us," Abinidab says, showing his dismay for the battle ahead of him.

"Father had me bring some food and I wanted to come out here to see how you were, but as I walked through the army, I noticed something strange. On the hill I heard our war cry, the war cry of certain victory from Yahweh. But then I see everyone standing still, even soiling themselves in the ranks. Why?" David says, extraordinarily frustrated.

"You know nothing about war David; you're a shepherd that plays a harp. Don't act like you know what to do, or that you could do better than these men. There are five men on the other side of the battlefield that are more horrifying than anything we have ever seen. Nephilim. And one of them, well, he is why the men are beside themselves with fear. His name is Goliath, the champion from Gath. Undefeated in battle, a warrior since his youth, and sharpened teeth because they say he loves to eat everything he fights before they are actually dead. He loves the sound of the screams of a man before he dies; he savors it as long as possible as he takes each bite of their flesh. He loves to--"

Just then, Goliath steps out of the ranks of Philistines and everyone stops talking. Quiet falls over the entire Ellah Valley. You can feel the fear and terror in every heart.

David starts to move toward the front of the battleline to see what they are all afraid of.

"David, get back here!" Abinidab shouts as quietly as possible, but David doesn't hear him.

As David is working his way through the men toward the front, he hears it: the most offensive thing he's ever heard out of another man's mouth to Yahweh. David's blood begins to boil as he hears the sound again, the same sound he heard when Samuel anointed him: the sound of a roaring lion. This time, however, it's not deafening; it's a distant sound, yet clearly present. David continues moving through the men, feeling like he is now being pulled forward by power in his veins, and as he gets to the last few rows of men he trips as they all turn back to run. David picks himself up and slowly locks eyes for the first time with a Nephilim. Every fiber of David's being is radiating with the power from Yahweh and the hatred for this race. David doesn't even blink as he stares into the eyes of Goliath across the battle line, everything in him longing to go destroy this creature like he did the lion and the bear. But then, David notices something interesting: Goliath doesn't seem to notice David staring at him. David hasn't moved, and is now the only Israelite in the Valley. Goliath laughs with his armor bearer, curses Yahweh one more time, and then turns back.

"It's true…" David says to himself, as he remembers the stories passed down from Caleb and Joshua about fighting giants. David has heard it said the Nephilim had bad eyesight due to their size, and thus the way to form an attack against them is by striking quick, lethal blows.

As David turns to walk back to the army, he sees all the men looking at him. Rather than feeling uncomfortable, David senses his destiny in that moment. He lets out a slight smile, savoring the moment as he walks in.

"One day, I will lead you all into battle as your king… One day," David says under his breath as he walks back to the men.

"Israel and the Philistines were drawing up their lines facing each other. David left his things with the keeper of supplies, ran to the battle lines and asked his brothers how they were. As he was talking with them, Goliath, the Philistine champion from Gath, stepped out from his lines and shouted his usual defiance, and David heard it. Whenever the Israelites saw the man, they all fled from him in great fear."
1 Samuel 17:21-24 NIV

Chapter Eight (b): Courage and confidence in chaos

"The only limit to our realization of tomorrow will be our doubts of today."
Franklin D. Roosevelt

If the opportunity to fulfill your dreams was presented today, would you be prepared like David was? The goal is to make sure your answer is the most confident yes you could ever give. A yes that you would risk your life on, a yes like David in the Valley of Elah, where his only response is longing to give the war cry before he sprints into a victorious battle. My goal is to help draw out of your heart a plan, a clear vision. and an understanding of "why" for your commitment to excellence moving forward. As you just read, I believe that when David saw the army out on the battlefield drawing the battle lines, it was a moment he had dreamed about for years. He wasn't flooded with insecurity; he was prepared and eager for his opportunity to put the power of God within him on display, because he knew what he was capable of. If you're willing to do some processing and deep diving in your soul, you can get to that same point, so that when your greatest moment of challenge and opportunity is presented, your Goliath, you will be so confident in your "yes, I have what it takes," you won't even think one second about the consequences of failure. You will say RAK CHAZAK, and sprint into the opportunity with your sling and five stones.

"You are never too old to set another goal or to dream a new dream."
C.S. Lewis

To begin, I need you to take some time today and reflect on this question. Find a place to be quiet, and spend 15-30 minutes in silence, meditating. This is one of the most important things we can do, so skipping this is not optional to fulfill this process.

Here's the question:

What dream do I have in my heart that I have allowed my circumstances, my age, my résumé, or the words of others to

affect, and make me believe victory is impossible?

Being honest with yourself, here and throughout your life, is mission-critical to the success of fulfilling the dreams the Lord has placed on your heart. Before moving forward, spend time in silent contemplation; when you're finished, write your answer down.

"Write the vision and make it plain on tablets, that he may run who reads it. For the vision is yet for an appointed time; but at the end it will speak, and it will not lie. Though it tarries, wait for it; because it will surely come, It will not tarry."
Habakkuk 2:2-3 NKJV

Now that you have an answer, we can move forward. If you feel embarrassed by what you wrote down, I urge you to never let your feelings about something define your faith in what you believe is possible. Feelings are a gift from God, but they were never created to be our master. We are created to walk by faith, not by sight. At the end of this book, I believe your feelings will begin to line up with the audacious faith you're going to develop in what you wrote down. Just imagine if you sat with young David, and heard him tell you that he believed he would be a great warrior for the Israelite Nation. We would all, without knowing the end of the story, think he was crazy. In love, most of us would try to help him navigate a solid 5-year plan for his life based on his current skill sets, his age, and current circumstance. Most of us wouldn't sit with him, hear his dreams, then begin mapping out a plan by faith from there. I fall in this category too many times, and I commit right now to change it. I want to be a dad that helps my kids dream big and make plans based on their dreams, rather than their current skill sets, age and circumstances. I want to be that for my wife as well. This can be taken out of context; most of us have seen the contestants on American Idol with dreams of being a big star but not an ounce of talent. We all feel heartbroken for those contestants when they show their loved ones pushing them forward, even though it was abundantly clear they didn't have any talent in that area. That is not love; that is fear of hurting someone's feelings. We need people who will take the time to get to know us, to see our true potential, and then fan that flame.

When my son says "Dad, I want to be Spiderman when I grow up" that's not a flame I fan. When he tells me, "Dad, I want to be an actor that does my own stunts," then I can analyze, process, and pray about the advice I give him and the opportunities I encourage him to take. I don't want him trying to fight Goliath if he has never fought the lion or the bear; I don't want him to sprint onto the battlefield with five stones if he has never used a sling. God is patient. This is a process of exploring the depth of your heart to see what dreams you believe God has placed there, because when God places a dream in your heart, it comes with the path to see your dream become your destiny. God wants to make sure that by the time the dream is fulfilled, we have the character and confidence to know our place. We don't want to end up like David when he was 50: a man that saw his dreams become a reality, but at some point lost his way. David's lust took over and destroyed the people he cared most about (2 Samuel 11). I believe living out our God-given dreams is one of the greatest gifts of living as children of God. God's dream for your life always includes preaching the Good News and making disciples. Whether you're a UFC fighter or an IT worker, the Great Commission is in the DNA of every God-given dream. This road is not the road to the "American Dream." This is the road to fulfilling God's dream for your life, and that road is full of landmines: making your dream an idol to be worshipped, discouragement warring for your soul to give up, and fiery arrows from the Enemy soaked in the flames of our temptations. We must make sure we walk, one step at a time, with extraordinary courage in the Spirit through the entire process.

"Be strong in the Lord and in his mighty power. Put on all of God's armor so that you will be able to stand firm against all strategies of the devil. For we are not fighting against flesh-and-blood enemies, but against evil rulers and authorities of the unseen world, against mighty powers in this dark world, and against evil spirits in the heavenly places. Therefore, put on every piece of God's armor so you will be able to resist the enemy in the time of evil. Then after the battle you will still be standing firm. Stand your ground, putting on the belt of truth and the body armor of God's righteousness. For shoes, put on the peace that comes from the Good News so that you will be fully prepared. In addition to all of these, hold up the shield

of faith to stop the fiery arrows of the devil. Put on salvation as your helmet, and take the sword of the Spirit, which is the word of God. Pray in the Spirit at all times and on every occasion. Stay alert and be persistent in your prayers for all believers everywhere."
Ephesians 6:10-18 NLT

I have a story to share, meant to illustrate how making a judgement based on my current ability would have destroyed my drive to see my dreams become a reality.

I will never forget the conversation my wife and I were having as we were driving to my first video shoot as a speaker; my wife was talking with me to see if I had rehearsed or done any prep work for what I was about to say. I was a little offended by her question; I had shared with her how I felt that God was going to use me to speak and write to people across the world. I wasn't sure why she wasn't cheering me on during our drive, hyping me up for my first shoot. I could tell she was genuinely concerned, because she knew something I didn't, and was trying to communicate it to me, but I was too ignorant to hear it. Ignorance does not generally lead to bliss; it leads to abrupt, hard realizations. We got to the studio, and my objective was clear: knock out a 30-second promotional video, and then my wife and I were headed out for a date with some friends. At this point I had spoken to a handful of live audiences and I felt ready to go...until I got in front of the camera. I completely froze up with what I wanted to say. It was the worst experience of my career. It took me four and a half hours to get a 30 second clip that wasn't even good; it was just complete. I left there devastated, and felt like David against the lion for the first time: questioning my dreams, my potential, my skill set, and pretty much everything in my life. My wife was gracious and empathetic, likely because I had just been publicly humiliated. If someone would have made a 5-year plan for my life in that moment, speaking, writing, and acting would have never been in that plan. That practical plan, probably done in the most loving way at the time, would have destroyed my dreams and taken me off the road to fulfill my destiny.

I had to process, pray, and meditate on my dreams that night, and I made a commitment to develop my ability to communicate in front of a camera. I began to practice every day with a camera we had at home (this was before smart phones); I would speak a topic into a camera, then send it to the best speaker I knew for feedback. It was a brutal process, but one I committed to no matter how painful the feedback was, because I knew I wanted to impact souls on the other side. Eventually that weakness became one of my biggest strengths. Now I am a full-time actor, author, and communicator. My favorite place to be professionally is in front of a camera when I hear the director say, "Action!"

I share that, and every story in this book, to inspire you to extraordinary courage in your everyday life. I want you to take what you have written down, what you believe to be your God-given dreams, and pretend you're seven years old again. Imagine that dream becoming a reality, imagine yourself standing like David against Goliath confident the victory was going to be his, and imagine the joy in your heart seeing yourself fulfill the dreams you wrote down today.

> *"Jesus looked at them intently and said, 'Humanly speaking, it is impossible. But with God everything is possible.'"*
> *Matthew 19:26 NLT*

David had a sling, stones, a shepherd's staff, and a harp to prepare him for the dreams God had placed in his heart. What do you have? If you have a dream to be an author, do you have a computer? That will be your sling, and your creativity your stones. Do you have a dream to be a social influencer? If you have a phone, you have your sling, and your content is your stones! Do you have a dream to be a UFC Champion? Grab your gloves and a bag. My favorite thing about any dream that God gives us is that He puts the sling, stones, staff and harp around us; we just have to use what we have in the moment to prepare us for the destiny for which we are fighting. Too many people allow over-analysis to cause paralysis in their soul, and they never take action because they are waiting for the perfect time. There will never be a perfect time to start preparing for your dreams, so don't look for it. Start moving forward with what you have, trusting that God will make provision for what you don't have. Let God show off in your life! Get to work with diligence and excellence on the path to see that dream become a reality. Work your butt off and ask God to use your offering to reveal Himself. Be encouraged and use your war cry in your training and pursuits; it's not the hope of victory, but the assurance of God's presence and perfect will!

RAK CHAZAK!

"Do you see a man who excels in his work? He will stand before kings; He will not stand before unknown men."
Proverbs 22:29 NKJV

Date

_____

Reflections

_____

_____

_____

_____

_____

_____

_____

_____

_____

_____

_____

_____

_____

_____

_____

_____

CHAPTER
NINE

The RAK
CHAZAK lifestyle

Walking back up to the men, David asks them, "What will be done for the man who kills this Philistine and removes this disgrace from Israel? Who is this uncircumcised Philistine that he should defy the armies of the living God?" 1 Samuel 17:26 NIV

One of the men in the army tells David, "The king will give great wealth to the man who kills him. He will also give him his daughter in marriage and will exempt his family from taxes in Israel." 1 Samuel 17:25 NIV

David smiles confidently, knowing that all he needs is a chance, "A chance to defeat an enemy of Yahweh, great wealth, a beautiful woman, and no taxes. Definitely not bad," David says quietly to himself.

When Eliab, David's oldest brother, heard him speaking with the men, he burned with anger at him and asked, "Why have you come down here? And with whom did you leave those few sheep in the wilderness? I know how conceited you are and how wicked your heart is; you came down only to watch the battle." 1 Samuel 17:28 NIV

"Now what have I done?" said David. "Can't I even speak?"
1 Samuel 17:29 NIV

David turns to the men next to him and asks them again to verify the reward promised. The men answered as before.

"David," one of the men says as he comes walking up to him. "The king wants to speak with you."

Eliab glares at David with disgust and says, "Don't dishonor our family,

96

redheaded shepherd baby."

A few of the men laugh, but David isn't fazed by the remark. Eliab has no idea that he is talking to a completely different man; a warrior king.

David follows the man that called him, leaving his brothers behind him. As they approach the king, these words seem to jump out of David's mouth to King Saul, "Let no one lose heart on account of this Philistine; your servant will go and fight him."
1 Samuel 17:32 NIV

Saul replied, "You are not able to go out against this Philistine and fight him; you are only a young man, and he has been a warrior from his youth." 1 Samuel 17:33 NIV

But David said to Saul, "Your servant has been keeping his father's sheep. When a lion or a bear came and carried off a sheep from the flock, I went after it, struck it and rescued the sheep from its mouth. When it turned on me, I seized it by its hair, struck it and killed it. Your servant has killed both the lion and the bear; this uncircumcised Philistine will be like one of them, because he has defied the armies of the living God. The Lord who rescued me from the paw of the lion and the paw of the bear will rescue me from the hand of this Philistine."
1 Samuel 17:34-37a NIV

Saul said to David, "Go, and the Lord be with you."
1 Samuel 17:37b NIV

"But before you go, put on the best armor in the land." Saul says to David.

David wanting to honor Saul says, "Yes sir."

Saul stands up, walks over to grab his armor then starts to put it on David. David, knowing the honor this was, didn't know how to tell the king that he didn't feel comfortable in his armor because he had never tested it. He continued to let the king dress him for battle in his armor.

Finally, David spoke up: "I cannot go in these," he said to Saul, "because I am not used to them." So he took them off."
1 Samuel 17:39 NIV

"David, what weapons are you going to use to fight Goliath?" Saul inquires of David.

"The weapons I know," David says as he grabs his staff and begins to walk toward the nearby stream.

"David," the king says, "RAK CHAZAK."

The moment David hears it, he knows this is not how this war cry is supposed to be used. Somewhere along the way, Saul lost the confidence of Yahweh's strength in battle. It reminded David of his war cry in the face of the lion the first time, when he ended up running away. Saying it with the hope of courage and strength, the hope of victory, but the fear of defeat in your heart.

David looks back at the king, "RAK CHAZAK!"

Everyone in the king's presence, including the king, is taken aback by the ferocity with which David spoke.

Before heading down to the stream, David takes one more look at the Philistine army, making sure his count is accurate.

"1... 2... 3... 4... 5. I was right. Five Nephilim. A stone for each..." David says to himself and then spits on the ground in disgust.

David walks down to the stream, enjoying the calm before the battle. It is time. He starts to sing one of his favorite songs as he selects the perfect stones for the five Nephilim.

"The Lord is my shepherd, I lack nothing. He makes me lie down in green pastures, he leads me beside quiet waters, he refreshes my soul. He guides me along the right paths for his name's sake. Even though I walk through the darkest valley, I will fear no evil, for you

are with me; your rod and your staff, they comfort me. You prepare a table before me in the presence of my enemies. You anoint my head with oil; my cup overflows. Surely your goodness and love will follow me all the days of my life, and I will dwell in the house of the Lord forever."
Psalms 23:1-6 NIV

As he finishes the song he loves, he drops the stones in his pouch, and stands still; he visualizes the great warlords Joshua and Caleb. He sees himself standing with them, in the calm before the battle.

"Yahweh, thank you for this opportunity," David says quietly.

As David leaves the stream, he makes eye contact with the filth of Gath, knowing he will soon be on the battlefield with him. David smiles, savoring every second, knowing victory from Yahweh is imminent. He walks through the men with his sling in his hand as his veins begin to boil with the power from Yahweh; he starts to hear the lion roar, and almost as if a volcano erupts from his mouth he shouts with ferocity the war cry of the Hebrew people through history,

"RAK CHAZAK!"

As if on cue, every man in the army, including David's brothers, shout back that ancient war cry that rumbled the valley,

"RAK CHAZAK!"

"So the Philistine came, and began drawing near to David, and the man who bore the shield went before him. And when the Philistine looked about and saw David, he disdained him; for he was only a youth, ruddy and good-looking. So the Philistine said to David, 'Am I a dog, that you come to me with sticks?' And the Philistine cursed David by his gods. And the Philistine said to David, 'Come to me, and I will give your flesh to the birds of the air and the beasts of the field!' Then David said to the Philistine, 'You come to me with a sword, with a spear, and with a javelin. But I come to you in the name of the Lord of hosts, the God of the armies of Israel, whom

you have defied. This day the Lord will deliver you into my hand, and I will strike you and take your head from you. And this day I will give the carcasses of the camp of the Philistines to the birds of the air and the wild beasts of the earth, that all the earth may know that there is a God in Israel. Then all this assembly shall know that the Lord does not save with sword and spear; for the battle is the Lord's, and He will give you into our hands.' So it was, when the Philistine arose and came and drew near to meet David, that David hurried and ran toward the army to meet the Philistine. Then David put his hand in his bag and took out a stone; and he slung it and struck the Philistine in his forehead, so that the stone sank into his forehead, and he fell on his face to the earth. So David prevailed over the Philistine with a sling and a stone, and struck the Philistine and killed him. But there was no sword in the hand of David. Therefore David ran and stood over the Philistine, took his sword and drew it out of its sheath and killed him, and cut off his head with it. And when the Philistines saw that their champion was dead, they fled."
I Samuel 17:41-51 NKJV

Chapter Nine (b): The RAK CHAZAK lifestyle

"What will be done for the man who kills this Philistine and removes this disgrace from Israel? Who is this uncircumcised Philistine that he should defy the armies of the living God?"
1 Samuel 17:26 NIV

One of the most important things I can share with you as we finish our journey together is this: it is not sinful for you to be excited about a reward for accomplishing your dreams. A reward for your hard work is a gift from God, and something to be fought for. I love that two times in scripture David asks what will be done for the man that kills Goliath. Wealth, a royal wife and no taxes?! That's a magnificent reward for a young man! Sometimes we over-spiritualize our answers, but I want to set you free from that. God longs to bless you; the Bible says God delights in it, and He wants to see the dreams He gave you fulfilled, because He knows the impact that will have in your life and the lives of others.

"Let them shout for joy and rejoice, who favor my vindication and want what is right for me; Let them say continually, 'Let the Lord be magnified, who delights and takes pleasure in the prosperity of His servant.'"
Psalms 35:27 AMP

"Hope deferred makes the heart sick, but a dream fulfilled is a tree of life."
Proverbs 13:12 NLT

Remember, any gift from God can become an idol in our heart if we don't walk in the Spirit. There is a constant war inside of us between the flesh and the Spirit (Galatians 5:16-17) and it is mission-critical that we are aware of it, and that we win that war daily. In the Spirit, there is no fear. In the Spirit, there are no idols. In the Spirit, we find every gift and every tool we need to accomplish our God-given mission and enjoy the fruit of our labor. In the Spirit, there is freedom and joy. In the Spirit, RAK CHAZAK becomes a lifestyle of knowing you have strength, courage, and victory in the Lord.

Our final step together is to take your dream (or dreams) and break it down into goals. Once we have this, we have the core ingredient that will make you push yourself in the gym, that will propel you forward with eating healthy, to get out of bed in the morning to spend intimate time with the Lord and His word, and to see every day as a training ground of preparation for the moment when your opportunity is presented. I believe having faith in a dream will give purpose to every difficult task of discipline we will face. Discipline is hard for everyone, but I believe it's impossible to sustain if you don't have a why for the pain you're enduring. I believe our God-given dream is our why, and it forces the how of the execution of the daily disciplines to fall into place, ensuring that when we show up in the Valley of Elah we are so confident in our preparation and so strong in our faith in the Lord's ability that we start asking what the reward is going to be!

I want you to take some time today and write down benchmarks to hit, twice a year, for four years. Make sure this is dreaming and planning with the Lord and not planning based on your current skill set. When my dream was to become an author, I set a goal for how many blogs I wanted to write in the first six months, and I had never blogged or written anything other than an email; I started, I figured out a way to launch a blog website, I created my first post, and I let my friends and family know about it. By the end of the first day I had 30 hits... as you can see, nobody will ever be able to say I was an overnight success. God has taken me through the long road of perseverance, but I am very grateful for it, even though it was definitely the valley of the shadow of death at times. It took me two years of blogging before I had a blog reach over a million people, and it was posted just after one of my worst-performing blogs to date. But I had a goal, a long-term dream, and that pushed me through every discouraging moment along the way. I believe it will for you as well. I will share an overview of my twice-a-year goals below, but first I want to share one of my all-time favorite quotes with you on this process:

"Start by doing what's necessary; then do what's possible; and suddenly you are doing the impossible."
St. Francis of Assisi

Here is an overview of my goals as an actor (I have them as an author as well). My acting journey started very similarly to where some of you might be at right now with your dream. It felt like it was something the Lord placed on my heart, and then I had to make a decision to have the courage to say RAK CHAZAK and sprint into the battle of obedience and growth. That was no joke. At this point I have worked with two incredible acting coaches, been trained by one of the best stunt choreographers in the world, read 32 acting books, had the honor to be the lead in a short film, and I'm currently cast as the lead in three indie action films. My 'yes' to what I felt the Lord was calling me to would have meant nothing without the RAK CHAZAK behind it: the war cry before you sprint headlong into the battle of preparation and obedience to the Lord.

My goal four years from now is to be the lead in a major action film in Hollywood.

From this point of my planning, I then take every 6 months and break down the practical side of what it's going to take on my end to see that dream become a reality. Like David against Goliath, I know the victory is only possible through God presenting the opportunity, giving me favor to seize it, being prepared, and the Spirit empowering me. My plan only succeeds if God shows up, and if my plan is off for some reason, I want what the Lord wants for my life. I want the success He wants, and I will learn contentment. Too many people say that while using their excuses as bricks to build their home of comfort and ease so they don't have to live with courage and take risks. I want you to join me to dream God-sized dreams and then take actions to see them come to pass. Remember: write your dream down, break it into 6-month chunks with a four-year completion date, and then you are finished with the foundation!

"I don't mean to say that I have already achieved these things or that I have already reached perfection. But I press on to possess that perfection for which Christ Jesus first possessed me. No, dear brothers and sisters, I have not achieved it, but I focus on this one thing: Forgetting the past and looking forward to what lies ahead, I press on to reach the end of the race and receive the heavenly prize

For me, being a lead in a major film in Hollywood is going to require the best version of myself as an actor: physically, mentally, emotionally, and spiritually. It's going to force me to leave behind my failures and successes to this point and give my all. I have promised myself this dream will not fail because of my lack of effort.

"It always seems impossible until it's done."
Nelson Mandela

Will you promise the same thing? I believe you have what it takes. I believe you are one of the ones that would walk onto the battlefield against Goliath, turn back to yell our war cry to inspire generations to watch and see what's possible when Christians live the RAK CHAZAK lifestyle! I believe we, and everyone that joins us, are going to inspire generations to come for the Kingdom of God. I hope our lives become stories that are legendary in the Kingdom, bringing glory to God and inspiration to every soul that hears them. I want you to know I am honored to be on this battlefield with you, giving our all for the King of kings!

RAK CHAZAK my friend, RAK CHAZAK!

"Be strong and courageous, for you are the one who will lead these people to possess all the land I swore to their ancestors I would give them. Be strong and very courageous. Be careful to obey all the instructions Moses gave you. Do not deviate from them, turning either to the right or to the left. Then you will be successful in everything you do. Study this Book of Instruction continually. Meditate on it day and night so you will be sure to obey everything written in it. Only then will you prosper and succeed in all you do. This is my command—be strong and courageous! Do not be afraid or discouraged. For the Lord your God is with you wherever you go."
Joshua 1:6-9 NLT

Date

_____

Reflections

_____

_____

_____

_____

_____

_____

_____

_____

_____

_____

_____

_____

_____

_____

_____

_____

_____

Thank you

It's my hope and prayer that this book impacted your life in a special way. This was the most unique writing experience of my career to this point. I felt like I poured my heart and soul into every paragraph and I loved every second.

As most of you know, I self-publish my books and the success of my writing depends on word-of-mouth. So I would be honored, if this book was a blessing to you, if you would help me spread the word. Texting a link to the book, sharing about the book on social media, or writing an Amazon review. Everything helps with getting this book out to as many people possible.

Thank you. Love and appreciate each of you more than you know!

Rak Chazak!

Cody Bobay

Other books by Cody Bobay
www.codybobay.com

Soulcon Challenge

Soulcon Warrior Elite

Date

_____

Reflections

_____

_____

_____

_____

_____

_____

_____

_____

_____

_____

_____

_____

_____

_____

_____

_____

_____

Date

Reflections

Date

Reflections

Date

Reflections

Date

Reflections

Date

Reflections

Date

Reflections

Date

Reflections